YOUTH AND
SOCIAL CHANGE

YOUTH AND SOCIAL CHANGE

RICHARD FLACKS

University of California
Santa Barbara

MARKHAM PUBLISHING COMPANY/Chicago

MARKHAM SERIES IN PROCESS AND CHANGE IN AMERICAN SOCIETY
Robert W. Hodge and David P. Street, Editors

Flacks, *Youth and Social Change*
Glaser, *Social Deviance*
Zald, *Occupations and Organizations in American Society:
The Organization-Dominated Man?*

ACKNOWLEDGMENTS

A great many people have helped in a great many ways in enabling me to write this book.

Much of the argument I make here is based on research I was involved in for several years at the University of Chicago. This research would never have gotten underway were it not for the intellectual initiative and material support of Professor Bernice Neugarten. It was her idea to merge my interest in student protest with her interest in intergenerational relations. The research operation could not have gone forward without the active participation of a remarkably talented collection of graduate students in sociology and human development. The following people did much of the data collection and most of the data analysis: Charles Derber, Paula Goldsmid, Patricia Schedler, Lillian Troll, Salma Angres, Charlotte Weissberg, and Eugene Thomas.

My intellectual debts are many. Professor Theodore Newcomb taught me much of what I know about student culture and how to study it. Kenneth Keniston's writing has been crucial in shaping my thinking about the characterological outcomes of contemporary childrearing and about "youth as a stage of life"—and I have, in addition, benefited from his encouragement. Jerome Skolnick and William Kornhauser provided intellectual and material opportunities to investigate the more macroscopic and historical dimensions of the American student movement. My thinking about the latter has been facilitated by the opportunity to collaborate with Milton Mankoff. As editors of the series of which this volume is a part, David Street and Bill Hodge provided the opportunity, freedom, and encouragement to bring much of my thinking together in a free-wheeling style.

Here at Santa Barbara, I have had a chance to know and learn from a great many students. Insights I have gained from conversations with them and from books and articles they have written permeate this book. I want to mention especially the following people who have helped me in more ways than they know: Joanne Frankfort, Mick Kronman, Jim Gregory, Bob Langfelder, Lon Ravitz, Phyllis Bennis, Ken Cruze, Chris Holverson, Liz Ferrera, Jeff Fazio, Bob Waters, Mark Muniz, Steve Lubarsky, Susan Wedow, Arnold Ross, Theo Majka, Eric Hutchins, and Ken Kenegos.

The basic source material for this book has been my involvement in the radical movement. It would be impossible to list all the people who have helped my understanding because I encountered them in and through the movement, but in the course of writing this I have benefited greatly from extensive talk with Paul Potter, Leni Wildflower, Carl Oglesby, Dick Magidoff, Rich Rothstein, and Bob Ross. I am particularly grateful to Norm Fruchter. My intellectual and spiritual debts to Tom Hayden are profound.

Three friends read drafts of this manuscript. Harvey Molotch helped me to understand its flaws at an early stage. Bill Glennon not only criticized a draft from a student's viewpoint, but has been, for me, a constant source of insight, criticism, and feedback. Todd Gitlin read and criticized the final draft. I have the feeling that much of this book is merely the record of the intense and prolonged conversations I have had with Bill and Todd. At a very deep level, the perspective of this book is the outcome of my relationship with my wife, Mickey. It is our shared experience that has helped me understand the process of achieving adulthood in these times, the problems of raising children and of womanhood, and the limitations as well as the strengths of "youth."

It is obvious that this book is dedicated to the rising generations—to those of us who have been young in these years, and to those, like my two small boys, whose lives depend on what we make of the future.

R. F.

CONTENTS

Series Introduction   ix

Introduction   1

1   The Idea of Youth   9

2   Growing Up Confused: Cultural Crisis and
Individual Character   20

3   Youth: An Unintended Consequence of Planned
Change   35

4   Youth As an Agency of Change: The Counterculture
and the Movement   47

5   Beyond the Youth Revolt: Some Possibilities for the
Seventies   104

Index   141

SERIES INTRODUCTION

In this volume on Process and Change in American Society—a series developed by Markham Publishing Company under our editorship—Richard Flacks provides an especially lucid account of how a new generation of American college youth transformed the placid campus of the 1950s into the politically responsive arena of the 1960s. They accomplished this transformation by injecting a measure of the dissent and partisan commitment that had been conspicuously absent (and without which dialogue turns into something more kindred to scripture reading than to a competition of ideas) and translating their discontent with the status quo into social action and social experimentation that reached beyond the university. Professor Flacks' perspective of these developments is admittedly and, in our view, refreshingly partisan. His treatment, although it is sympathetic to the radical youth movement, is hardly the result of blind devotion. Rather, it is firmly based on research and a critical reassessment of the strategies for action adopted by the movement over the course of its continuing evolution. One need not share Professor Flacks' commitments to learn a great deal about the role of youth, especially of middle class college youth, in the political and social developments of the 1960s.

The future of the radical youth movement that developed on college campuses during the 1960s is uncertain. Remember that the noise on campus was often, but not always, created by a small minority of students. Many of the young adults who eschewed activism nevertheless continued quietly to prepare themselves for traditional careers, and thousands more entered the labor market and the process of family formation directly from secondary school without having been exposed to the campus scene. Obviously, many youths are already established in the life cycle pattern of older generations and are undoubtedly as recalcitrant to fundamental transformation of our society as were their elders. Furthermore, even youths who are radical sometimes revert to the conservatism of old age and of their social position when they leave the campus. Despite these factors, to judge the radical youth movement of the 1960s inconsequential is premature. As Professor Flacks observes in his concluding chapter, the radical youth movement contains numerous possibilities for transcending itself and profoundly affecting the future course of American society. Even now it is clear that campus activities of the 1960s have increased the variety of life courses open in our society. At least a young professional now has options that enable him to devote his life to the service of others—options that largely were not available ten years ago. Furthermore, a greater variety of personal relationships between the sexes is tolerated, and the idea that the measure of a person's moral worth is exhausted by his monetary value has been eroded substantially.

Admiration of radical youth is by no means universal because youth has failed to bring out the best in many of us and revealed the worst in some of us. It is frightening to see distinguished scholars who are presumably committed to intellectual freedom and dissent respond to the inquiries and protests of youth by labeling them fascists and psychotics. No one likes to field questions he cannot answer and it requires no new principles of psychology to understand why in these situations even distinguished men may respond defensively and revert to authoritarianism. Similarly, no one likes to have his questions evaded or given precoded answers, and it requires no new principles to understand why inquiring youth might flaunt authorities who discredit themselves through displays of threat rather than of reason. To be sure, radical campus rhetoric is often more vacuous than incisive, but that is perhaps a greater indictment of the failure of higher education than of the students who produced it. It is also easy to dismiss the disruption of the university by youth as a violation of the rights of others to pursue their work and studies within the established regime. Undoubtedly, there is truth to this claim, but it should be tempered by an awareness that the rights of some may be secured by appropriating the freedom of others.

Although we do not share Professor Flacks' commitment to and sympathy with the radical youth movement, we do feel that the movement has raised significant questions about our society and that the trouble on campus ultimately must be traced to the organization of higher education and its place in society rather than attributed to the whims and perversions of a few rebellious youth. Explanations based on the wickedness of men only provide the ideological justification for repression; those based on the wickedness of institutional arrangements hold forth the promise of a good society. Radical students have often better understood this principle than have their intellectual elders, who have also been reluctant to grasp the idea that universities and other social institutions cannot exist *in* a society without being *of* it.

In developing this series, we have encouraged the authors to use systematic and quantitative materials wherever they are available. We have also encouraged them to use alternative sources to fill in the appreciable gaps that are left by the quantitative record. Perhaps, most important, we have encouraged the authors to present their material in a provocative way, tying together the scraps of statistical and documentary evidence with a theoretical viewpoint, a central theme, or even a critical perspective informed by articulated ideological principles. Richard Flacks' moving evaluation and commentary on events that have already touched most of us and may well affect our lives for years to come admirably fulfills that charge.

Robert W. Hodge
University of Michigan

David P. Street
State University of New York
at Stony Brook

November, 1971

INTRODUCTION

Hardly a day passes without publication of another book or major magazine article on the "youth." If journalists, intellectuals, social scientists, and many others feel compelled to describe, analyze, advocate and attack the activities of the young, many laymen feel compelled to read these reports. I think the most fundamental source of the hunger for explanation is that in various ways young people are attacking or moving away from the main cultural, political and social institutions and principles of American society; moreover, they are doing so at a time of unprecedented material abundance and individual opportunity. Many Americans can understand revolt—especially when it takes place in other lands or in other eras—but we tend to understand it as a response to hunger, tyranny and gross inequality. What seems to be so incomprehensible about the youth revolt, especially the protest of white middle class youth, is that it is being carried on by well-fed Americans who seem to have bright personal futures in an economic sense, are surrounded by luxurious goods, and have, if anything, too much freedom. Apparently, this is incomprehensible. Something new is happening: a movement that seems to have no identifiable origins is threatening the established way of life. It cannot be rationalized so it must be explained away.

You have a right to be bored with the idea of reading still another book about the subject, but you might share my feeling that most reports and explanations are profoundly inaccurate and incomplete. Perhaps you also share my conviction that what is happening among young people is sufficiently significant, deep, and complex to warrant continuous efforts to clarify, revise, and extend our interpretations of the subject.

I cannot claim to offer anything here that is less unsatisfactory or more valid than are the ideas and theories you may have read or those that you yourself have thought about or discussed with your friends. I can comment about what I've tried to do in this book and explain the particular vantage point from which I have written.

As a student who went to college in the fifties, I was "deviant" because I was something of a political activist. As president of the campus Young Democrats, I circulated petitions supporting civil rights legislation, attended meetings, and passed out a lot of leaflets. Of some 10,000 students on my campus, perhaps 50 of us were politically active: that 50 included all the Young Democrats, Young Republicans, Young Socialists, Young ADAers, Student NAACPers, and student government politicians that there were. Usually, our efforts to persuade students to sign civil rights petitions were met with the response that signing or joining anything "might jeopardize the government job I'm planning to get." In short, it was a time of almost total political apathy, produced, at least in part, by a fear that taking any kind of stand on any issue might get you into trouble. This attitude pervaded the 1950s. It was rooted in the fear of McCarthyism—the widespread practice of relentless investigation and blacklisting of people who had been classed as radicals and liberals during the Depression and World War II periods.

I remember not only the apathy of the fifties, but the virtual miasma of blandness that engulfed student life during those years. Blandness was expressed in the way students looked—the crew-cuts, the Ivy League charcoal gray clothes, the bermuda shorts, and the circle pins. And underneath the apathy and the blandness was the sense that everyone was trying to "make it"—into a secure, "privatized," corporate and suburban niche.

A few of us were politicos and "intellectuals." That is, we felt that we were set apart from the overwhelming majority of students by our concern: we cared about society, about art, about books, and about ideas. Nevertheless we shared with the majority a pretty strong cynicism. The future would, we expected, look pretty much like the fifties. The best we could hope to achieve was a way of life that would be reasonably enriching spiritually, interesting, and principled. For me and for most of my friends, academic life offered one of the few opportunities to do interesting work, meet interesting people, and exchange ideas with others who shared the same intellectual interests, without the restrictions imposed by time clocks. So I decided to go to graduate school and become a social scientist.

Beginning in 1960, at least in Ann Arbor where I was doing graduate work, some new developments on the campus were evident. More and more students were actively demonstrating in support of the southern civil rights movement. The atmosphere of blandness and conventionalism was being replaced by a climate of increasingly freewheeling political debate. An increasing number of students were being bound together by their common interest in folk music, serious filmmaking, and other avant-garde cultural activities and were experimenting with a definitely bohemian style of dress and living.

In 1962, I became aware of a group of students in Ann Arbor who were seriously considering the creation of a national movement of students for basic social change. They were forming an organization called "Students for a Democratic Society" and making serious plans to mobilize student participation in the civil rights movement and in the growing national campaign against nuclear testing and the arms race. To me, the birth of SDS seemed to portend that, unexpectedly, times were changing—McCarthyism was dead and campus apathy and conformity were being challenged by a new spirit of commitment and dissent. Eagerly, I joined SDS, took part in its founding national convention, was elected to its national executive committee, and thereby was changed from a cynical expolitico into a young "new radical."

Since then, I have remained an active participant in the movement—for several years as an officer of SDS, later, as a faculty member organizing teach-ins against the war, supporting student demonstrations, and making endless speeches. In reading what I have written, keep in mind that aspect of my experience and commitment. My involvement has given me firsthand knowledge of both the participants and the operations of the movement that few of its interpreters have enjoyed, but my commitment surely biases my interpretation of the youth revolt as positive, as historically decisive (rather than as marginal), and as socially necessary.

During these same years I became a sociologist. That is, in addition to developing a partisan commitment, I developed a professional commitment—to improve my own understanding of social phenomena and to impart that understanding to others. The emergence of the student movement in the sixties stimulated my curiosity as a sociologist as well as my allegiance as a human being. Why, for instance, should the change in campus climate from the fifties to the sixties have been so marked? Who were these people who started SDS? Who were the new troubadours and poets who were learning how to combine the pop and the serious in such surprising ways? Why were well-fed, privileged youths putting themselves on the line for racial equality and abolition of war and the draft? And why were both the troubadours and the activists winning increasing support and following among wider and wider circles of young people? These were questions of sociological centrality. They bore on matters that sociologists had been addressing in recent years. Indeed, generally, they had not only failed to predict the mass movements of the sixties, but their theoretical perspectives had tended to deny the very possibility that such movements could, in fact, occur at all in a "stable," "democratic," "pluralist," "affluent" society like the United States.

Accordingly, I have been involved for the past seven years in various forms of research and analysis of student protest and youth culture—as a sociologist. In the mid-sixties, a group of colleagues and I at the University of Chicago (where I was then teaching) undertook one of the first studies of the social backgrounds of new left activists—a study involving extensive interviews with fifty activists and their parents, and a comparable number of nonactivist students and their parents. Since that time, I have collected a diverse array of survey data on the social origins of activists as well as on their ideological and personal perspectives. In addition, I have tried over the years to be a participant-observer —to collect and record impressions and experiences from the vantage point of the onlooker, while at the same time working as an engaged member of a variety of organizations and communities related to the movement and the counterculture. To a high degree, this essay represents a summary of, and a reflection on, the "data" I have thus acquired.

Unquestionably, there is some tension between professional and partisan commitments. Commitment to partisan goals implies a dedication to the triumph in society of particular cherished values, while commitment to professional ends connotes a dedication to the use of rational and objective methods in pursuit of truth, regardless of the consequences.

Without arguing the point, I contend that partisanship and professionalism can be mutually supportive. The professional-partisan who maintains both commitments may be in a position to probe more deeply, scrutinize more carefully, and be more sensitive to certain ranges of experience than the professional who has tried to remain aloof from political engagement is able to be. Furthermore, the aloof stance may be an unconscious (or conscious) cover for concealed allegiances to the status quo. On the other hand, the rational, objective, truth-telling stance of the ideal professional is a spirit that, in my opinion, ought to be alive in any social movement that has humanistic goals. The fusion of these stances is what I try for here; nevertheless you should be alert to the ways in which this fusion fails. For instance, how do my biases seem to distort interpretation, create blind spots, and so forth. On the other hand, how does a rationalistic, objective tone tend to miss the passion, the experiential richness, and the mystery of what is being described?

In any case, what is the objective of this essay? First, it assumes that both a student movement and a youth counterculture did indeed develop during the past decade and that these developments were new in American society. They were new, first of all, in that there is no precedent in American history for either a radical movement of such intensity and extensivity developing on the campus, or for young people in such numbers to define themselves in substantial opposition to the established culture. There is a long history of radicalism in America (although rarely embodying such revolutionary rhetoric and practice), but never before has a movement been conceived by and composed of youth as such; there is a history of student radicalism (though never so militant or so extensive), but typically, it identified with, and was generated by, adult organizations and parties. There is a history of youthful bohemianism in America, but its previous manifestations have been confined to relatively tiny groups of young people.

It is important to keep in mind that revolutionary student movements and generational conflict have been widespread and endemic phenomena in many parts of the world. Nevertheless, until the sixties, such movements have been regarded as characteristic of underdeveloped, agrarian-based societies that are undergoing modernizing pressure under autocratic regimes—Russia, China, Latin America, and nineteenth century Germany, for example—not of advanced, industrial, democratic societies. So this is another aspect of the newness of these movements—they are occurring in unexpected times and places, and under conditions that seem quite inconducive to their growth.

The basic theoretical perspective taken here is that the revolt of youth is a *symptom* of a fundamental sociocultural crisis. In general terms, the crisis involves a substantial conflict between the emergent technological potentialities of a society and the established social order and cultural system. If the technological capacities of the system are to be realized, new values, new motivational patterns, new rights, and new institutions must be established. Technological changes have created new social roles—new classes—whose occupants experience discontent with old ways and established structures. Institutional and cultural evolution proceeds as the result of countless efforts by countless individuals to adapt to new problems, to adopt new ways, and to realize new aspirations. There is a prolonged crisis because by and large, the established political system and authority structure resists major change. In this situation, increasing numbers of youth regard the culture as incoherent and the future as undesirable and chaotic. Young people are among the first to experience this sense of crisis because they have yet to form stable vocational and social attachments, because they receive most directly and fully the socializing efforts of established institutions, and because they are future-oriented. For many youths in this situation, the cultural crisis is experienced as a crisis of identity—an inability to define the meaning of one's life and to accept the meanings and models of adulthood offered by parents and other elders.

But identity crisis and discontent by themselves do not account for *collective* revolt. The formation of social movements and subcultures requires that those who are restless be available to each other for mutual influence and common action. Consequently, I argue that the same circumstances that have created a crisis for youth have also created the environmental framework for their coming together. The discontent and the coming together are also separate, somewhat distinct processes. Thus, an understanding of what has been happening collectively among young people cannot rest on explanations referring to discontent alone or on explanations simply referring to mutual influence.

One of the important questions about mass movements is why only a portion of their potential base of support actually participates actively in them. Moreover, one often discovers—and this has been especially true of the youth movements of the sixties —that movement activists are recruited primarily from a rather special and isolated segment of the larger and more heterogeneous population that the movement is addressing. Any explanation of the movements of the past decade must account for the fact that they were initiated by a *definite type of youth* that is quite different from the majority of young people in terms of social background, values, interests, and aspirations. Why was this the case? And, since the movements spread far beyond the ranks of this initiating type—how was it possible for a group of "deviants" to influence the previous conventional and hostile majority?

Finally. Can we say anything about the future? Based on our reading of the ways in which movements interact with established authorities and existing institutions, can we describe probable trends for the next decade? Given such trends, can we find clues to the means by which we in the present can shape the future so that it has some resemblance to our dreams?

This essay tries to deal with all of these matters in a brief and sometimes sketchy fashion. Given my experiences, research and background, I have found it necessary to exclude some issues of great importance. In particular, I have been unable to write with any authority on the situation and action of black and other third world youth. Similarly, I have failed to come to grips systematically with the problems of working class white youth. Thus, what you will read here is woefully "ethnocentric" (as is much of academic sociology and contemporary white radicalism). Nevertheless, I could not bring myself to theorize about matters that were beyond my direct experience. As a result, the analysis developed here is bound to be partial and inadequate.

Still, if I, as a white, relatively young, middle class, intellectual have helped other young, white, middle class people understand how their individual lives relate to larger historical processes, that is about the best I can hope to do. Part of that understanding includes the recognition of the extreme isolation of white middle-class youth from millions who have even more stake in a future alternative to that which is presently programmed than we have.

Since many who will read this know more about what is being discussed than I do (although they may not be credentialed "experts"), I would be most grateful for their reactions—however critical.

1
THE IDEA OF YOUTH

Puberty is a biological fact, but youth is a social one. There is no biological imperative to reinforce the idea that for several years after puberty young persons should continue to be segregated from adults and prevented from assuming adult sexual, economic, and social roles. By age 18, at the latest, virtually everyone is physiologically adult, having reached sexual maturity and the peak of physical and mental capacity. Thus, the segregation and categorization of young people is unknown in many cultures; furthermore, it is a very recent development in western civilization. Philippe Ariès, the historian of childhood, documents that

> in the Middle Ages, at the beginning of modern times, and for a long time after that in the lower classes, children were mixed with adults as soon as they were considered capable of doing without their mothers or nannies, not long after a tardy weaning (in other words, at about the age of seven). They immediately went straight into the great community of men, sharing in the work and play of their companions, young and old alike. . . . As soon as he had been weaned, or soon after, the child became the natural companion of the adult.

In terms of age, it seems convenient to say that childhood ends at age 13, that adolescence covers the years from 13 to 16, and that youths are persons over 16 who have not yet entered the labor force as full-time participants. The idea that children are not ready for participation in adult life and require a period of separation and preparation to be made ready has held increasing sway in our culture for nearly two centuries. However, it should not be forgotten that only during the last five decades have the principles of compulsory schooling and exemption from labor been extended to working-class as well as to high-status children.

The restriction of adolescents is an even more recent concept. In the year 1900, less than 100,000 of the 1.5 million 17 year olds had completed high school. Not until 1940 did the proportion of adolescents who had completed twelve years of school reach 50 percent, and only in the last decade have at least 66 percent of teenagers completed high school. Obviously, these figures indicate that until the beginning of World War II, adolescents were not normally segregated; moreover, until that time, most persons 16 years and over were considered to be adults or full-time workers. If we define "youth" as that stage of life coming after adolescence but prior to full-time participation in work roles, most people in our society could not have experienced such a stage of life until the present decade.

Today, for the first time in history, less than half of the people between 16 and 21 are full-time members of the labor force. A large proportion is still in school. A fraction is in the armed forces. A very substantial number is unemployed, marginally employed, or in the streets. Furthermore, of those between 21 and 24 years old, 25 percent, an unprecedented figure, are still in school. Substantial separation of the typical person under 25 from adult life and roles is a development of the past ten years. It is one of the most important social developments of the years since World War II. There have been "youths" throughout history, but as far as one can tell, never has such a large proportion of the young population been so "youth"-ful.

Because the transitional period between childhood and adulthood is a byproduct of the extension of formal schooling its development has been largely intentional. Formal education is a social requisite to the extent that the family by itself cannot adequately prepare children for adult roles. To the extent that a socioeconomic order contains roles that require highly developed and specialized skills and embodies some degree of competition based on merit and achievement in order to take such roles, parents and other relatives must be replaced by educational specialists to prepare at least a fraction of the young for adulthood. The proportion of young in school and the length of time they are expected to remain there are greatly increased as industrial society evolves because this type of society requires that its members have an unprecedented degree of flexibility and mobility. The process of creating new types of work and phasing out old lines is continuous; the need for universal discipline, literacy, specialized training, and meritocratic competition steadily widens.

Historically, the masses of young have been "desegregated" as they have reached physiological adulthood. Traditionally, the continued segregation and education of physiological adults have universally been restricted to the male offspring of the elite (plus a handful of nonelite youths who seemed especially suited for elite roles). As a stage of life, then, youth has been regarded as a necessary and desirable goal only for those who were born to rule or who have been selected to govern or to serve as high caretakers of the established culture. This degree of education was regarded as necessary not only for attainment of intellectual sophistication, but also for development of the characterological refinement appropriate to an elite.

Thus, as societies have become increasingly complex, differentiated, industrialized, and bureaucratized, the segregation and categorization of young persons seems to have been an intended and invariable feature of their evolution, applauded as an element of "progress" and as manifestly "functional" for the going culture. Moreover, those who have held power in such societies typically have wanted their own sons to become "youths" in this sense, viewing such an additional preadult stage as particularly valuable for sustaining or enhancing the status of the family name.

But the development of higher schooling for young adults has often had certain dramatically unintended consequences for the elites who have sponsored it. Periodically, in many parts of the world, these educated youths have joined together in active opposition to those elites and to the established order that they were being educated to uphold and strengthen.

At the risk of some simplification, we can say that there is a kind of classic pattern of factors that gives rise to a mass student movement opposed to the established order. The heart of the matter is that a university system has been introduced into a backward society. The rulers of such a society regard the university system as a vehicle that will enable qualified members of their society to take advantage of the technical, scientific, and intellectual advances of "modern" society. This future elite will be able to hold its own in relation to the elites of more advanced countries without disturbing the cultural framework, structure of privilege, and political order of backwardness.

Historically, the hope that higher education will have a modest, controlled, gradual impact on backward societies has proved false. (As I use the term here, societies are backward—including those of nineteenth century Germany, Russia, and eastern Europe; China and other Asian countries; and most of Latin America—in the following sense: agriculture, as the primary mode of production, dominates the society; a feudal and aristocratic structure of power and privilege prevails; and the culture is religiously and traditionally oriented.) In preindustrial backward societies, the prevailing system was weakened under the impact of pervasive corruption, aggression from the industrializing, expansionist West, the rise of indigenous elements favoring capitalism, and the introduction of modern western ideas and values. Inevitably, the universities embodied and disseminated the newest ideas and values. They inculcated such values as scientific, legal, and civil rationality and introduced students to concepts of equality, democracy, liberty, and nationalism. Meanwhile, many students were hungry for new cultural perspectives. They sensed the obsolescence and ineffectuality of their fathers and the values represented by the parent generation. At first, most students felt they could implement the modern ideas they were acquiring by appealing to the established elites on the one hand and using the elite positions they would inherit on the other. Classically, student movements began when both such expectations were frustrated.

Obviously, resistance of the established regime to proposals for reform is a major impetus to the formation of mass student opposition. The typical regime was not only unresponsive but positively repressive toward such pressures. As students began to appeal for reform, censorship was imposed, police surveillance was intensified, and dissidents were punished and jailed. The dis-affected young became increasingly aware of the enormous gap between their acquired ideals and the social and political condition of their country. At the same time, their awareness of the scanda-lous lack of morality demonstrated by established elites who were incapable of living up to their own professed moral values became heightened.

Educated youths in backward countries were faced with not only political intransigence, corruption, and decay, but with the knowledge that their own personal futures were dubious, to say the least. Invariably, backward societies overproduce educated youth in the sense that career opportunities commensurate with their training were inadequately provided. There were simply not enough positions available for the hundreds of new lawyers, scholars, and intellectuals who had graduated. In a short time, the ranks of the student youth were swelled by a growing mass of declassed and deeply discontented unemployed intelligentsia con-centrated in the cities.

Disillusioned with the established order and the parent gen-eration, students and exstudents quite often sought links with peas-ants and other sectors of the poor. This impulse was reinforced by a rising spirit of nationalism, which crystallized a sense of identification with the people of the nation against the corrupt rulers and the elders of society. Especially in the early stages of student radicalization, however, the average citizen was rarely responsive because of the heavy weight of traditional culture and economic necessity on the consciousness of the masses. Conse-quently, students and intelligentsia were obliged to rely on mem-bers of their own narrow circles as principal catalysts of change. It is this situation that produced the paradox found in many backward nations: the masses were depressed and deprived, but the primary initiative for struggle against the status quo emanated primarily from the young intelligentsia who were more materially advantaged. Student activism was facilitated by the freedom afforded students. As a group protected by the traditional university autonomy partially accepted even by very authoritarian regimes, students often were the only group free to organize political dissent. Since students were offspring of the elites, it was relatively hard to use methods of brutal suppression against them. To brutalize students of elite status was always more damaging to the regime than to brutalize peasants or urban mobs.

Finally, student solidarity was promoted by student proximity; they were segregated into enclaves that permitted intimate association and mutual identification under conditions of *both* repression *and* relative freedom and they were privileged but lived in considerable poverty and economic insecurity.

These were the conditions, then, that classically gave rise to mass student movements—movements expressing nationalist and populist identification with the poor, deep hostility toward the parent generation, strong convictions of the moral righteousness and redemptive character of the fraternity of the young, and a longing for a new culture based on principles of brotherhood, community, expressive freedom, and equality. In some cases, such movements have succeeded in toppling regimes through their own mass action. In other cases—especially in the case of Russia, China, and Vietnam—such movements provided the men who eventually organized and led successful revolutionary parties that won the allegiance of the masses. Indeed, although student movements rarely achieve their aspirations through the efforts of students acting as students, almost always, they constitute the breeding ground for those who will eventually lead broader mass movements of nationalist, reformist, or revolutionary character.

In any case, the emergence of student and youth movements in backward societies has been a definite omen of the collapse of traditional culture, a very important indicator that major upheaval and societal transformation is impending. In such societies, in other words, *the emergence of sharp generational conflict and the mass uprising of privileged youth signify that a certain stage of social development is coming to an end and a new one is taking form.* The new stage when it arrives, may not resemble the future the students themselves had in mind; indeed, the students who so frequently catalyze a process of qualitative social change may not play much role in shaping the outcomes of that process.

If student movements have historically been forerunners of the breakdown of traditional culture, it is easy to see why they have not been significant factors in the history of the United States and England, for example. These and other capitalist democracies were industrialized early and did not have to overcome the profound entrenchment of traditional culture, feudal organization, and despotism. In Marxian terms, those societies that contained within themselves a strong indigenous bourgeoisie to carry the spirit and practice of modernization did not require a university system to function as the principal center of opposition to traditional culture. In these societies, the established culture was already rationalistic, democratic, and otherwise modern when the universities began to assume any central social significance. Consequently, most university students in such societies have been conservative, fully integrated into the established order, and ready to assume elite roles without significant strain (in the United States, for example). Generational revolt in these societies has been virtually absent; typically, youths who have felt estranged or radical have expressed their dissatisfaction not by revolt of the *youth,* but by joining movements of political reform and cultural renovation led by *adults.* Tension between parents and offspring, although common, has been expressed only rarely through social conflict and mass movement; rather, the young have achieved independence from their elders by striking out on their own, using the opportunities for geographical and social mobility which were widely available. In short, as Lewis Feuer suggests, American society has historically been characterized by "generational equilibrium." No doubt such equilibrium is attributable to the fact that American culture has historically been regarded as progressive, open, and viable by each new generation of educated youth. Such youth did not regard their parents as hopelessly backward. They did not conceive the political regime as hopelessly unresponsive or repressive. They did not experience an enormous gap between the values they acquired at home or in schools and those upheld by political and institutional elites. They did not experience vocational blockage, but instead looked forward to upward mobility. To the extent that they perceived social injustice and political corruption, they also experienced widespread opposition to such conditions in adult society.

Since the above argument risks misinterpretation, let me clarify one point. Many Americans *have* experienced American society as repressive, unjust, and corrupt. But they have responded to that experience not as *youth,* but as Indians, blacks, workers, and farmers, for example. Since its inception, American society has experienced extensive and militant protest and rebellion, but rarely, if ever, has such activity been carried on by those who defined themselves as youths (even if many of those who have been most active in such struggles have tended to be young). Meanwhile, the number of persons in this society who can be defined as youths (that is, physiologically adult or late adolescents who are not performing adult roles) has been increasing steadily. But most of these young people have not had a sharp sense of collective consciousness or a sense of themselves as being involved in collective rebellion.

It is fair to say that equilibrium rather than conflict has been the dominant theme in generational relations in the United States. Presumably this is so because on the one hand, there has been an essential consistency between social structural and cultural factors in the society and on the other hand, social conflict has relatively freely been carried on along class, ethnic, and other interest group lines.

However, evidence of collective youth revolt within the framework of equilibrium has not been entirely absent. For instance, since the beginning of the twentieth century in America, a few educated, middle class youths have openly broken with the dominant culture and participated in bohemian communities and lifestyles. Most of the artists, writers, bohemians, and rebels who emigrated to Greenwich Village before World War I and to Paris during the twenties defined themselves as youths, identified their struggle against prevailing values in generational terms, and resembled their counterparts in preindustrial societies. Moreover, their attacks on bourgeois values, their defense of the avant-garde against the traditional, and their visions of a new cultural framework had a steadily widening impact on American consciousness. During the 1930s, American universities experienced not only an increase in student bohemianism, but also a considerable outburst of student political radicalism that was expressed through antiwar protests and support for communist and socialist parties and ideologies.

For some fifty years, then, a segment of American youth has been attracted to either bohemianism or radicalism or both. During these decades, however, relatively few youths were involved and the generational content of their revolt, although present, was rarely expressed in very sharp terms. Student radicals *in particular* have always felt themselves to be allied with adult movements and parties. Rarely have they acted as youth independent of, and opposed to, the interests and influences of older generations. By the 1950s, it appeared to most observers that the minor tradition of youthful rebellion in America had come to an end, drowned in affluence, career opportunity, the moral failure of ideological politics, and the impact of the cold war on American political and cultural life. Most observers at the time argued that the inherent stability, flexibility, and openness of the American sociopolitical system and the broad American value consensus were deeply rooted and would engulf and absorb movements of opposition, especially when these were rooted in the alienation of only a small number of young intellectuals.

Events of the sixties disproved these predictions. The relations between young people and the society at large have been qualitatively transformed.

First, a *general* "youth culture" that attracts the interest and participation of young people of many social strata and geographic regions has emerged for the first time in our history. Previously, the culture that separated the adolescent and youth population from adult roles was segmented into a variety of discrete subcultures and styles. During the past decade, young people of many types have increasingly come to share an overarching common set of symbols and attitudes. To be sure, distinct differences distinguish the white middle class youth culture from black ghetto youth culture, but even these cultures share some common symbols and sometimes seek alliances with each other.

Moreover, the new national youth culture, unlike the "teenage" expressions of the thirties, forties, and fifties, contains strong elements of explicit opposition to the prevailing adult culture. Significantly, many of its active spokesmen see the youth culture not as a transitional experience, but as a *counter*culture—that is, a definite challenge to the values and norms that are officialy proclaimed and institutionalized in the larger society.

Second, during the past decade, youth has engaged in oppositional radical and revolutionary politics on a scale never before experienced in this country. Moreover, it has done so *as youth,* with little or no adult control or guidance, and with a strong component of antipathy to adult politics of any variety.

Here, then, is the heart of the issue. Before the 1960s, not only laymen, but also social scientists viewed American society as highly stable—a society in which values, institutions and technological requirements were basically well meshed. This society has been described as a uniquely open society—one that is responsive both to the aspirations and demands of the people and to the need for change.

Nevertheless it is now experiencing precisely that sort of social convulsion that has always been reserved for societies characterized by extreme cultural incoherence and social rigidity. Youth countercultures, student movements, and other expressions of generational revolt occur when societies undergo processes of cultural breakdown. Such cultural crises have typically been evident when traditional values, meanings, and norms appear to be obsolete, retrogressive, or incoherent to an increasing number of members of a society. Usually these crises are symptomatic of the fact that technological change has rendered traditional practices and institutions irrelevant and has generated a spreading pattern of new hopes, expectations, and demands. These new aspirations are, however, not met by existing institutions and by the established structure of authority. Indeed, they are often actively resisted and repressed by those who have power.

If this analysis has validity—if it is true that in other societies the emergence of youth revolt is an important symptom of cultural breakdown—then perhaps the same is true for us. It seems plausible that the picture of America as a stable, open society needs drastic revision.

During the past several decades, this society must have been experiencing a pattern of change that threatened the stability of the cultural framework that previously provided young people with a sense of purpose, meaning, and confidence in the future. In Chapters 2 and 3, I analyze the main themes of that pattern. What was it that prepared the ground for the youth uprising of the sixties?

BIBLIOGRAPHICAL NOTES

1. The concept of youth developed here is based on a paper by Kenneth Keniston, "Historical Process and Psychological Development: Youth as a Stage of Life," mimeographed (New Haven, Conn.: Yale Medical School, 1969); Philippe Ariès, *Centuries of Childhood* (New York: Vintage, 1965); David Matza, "Position and Behavior Patterns of Youth," in R. E. Faris (ed.), *Handbook of Modern Sociology* (Chicago: Rand McNally, 1964); Bennett Berger, *Looking for America* (Englewood Cliffs, N. J.: Prentice-Hall, 1971).

2. Statistics on trends in schooling of youth were based on data reported in Bureau of the Census, *Statistical Abstracts of the United States* (Washington, D. C.: Bureau of the Census, 1969, 1970).

3. On the social functions of higher education, see Christopher Jencks and David Riesman, *The Academic Revolution* (Garden City, N. Y.: Doubleday, 1968); Joseph Ben-David and Randall Collins, "A Comparative Study of Academic Freedom and Student Politics," in Seymour Martin Lipset (ed.), *Student Politics* (New York: Basic Books, 1967), 148–195.

4. The discussion of "classical" student movements is based on Ben-David and Collins, *op. cit.;* Smuel N. Eisenstadt, *From Generation to Generation* (Glencoe, Ill.: Free Press, 1956); Seymour Martin Lipset, "University Students and Politics in Underdeveloped Countries," in S. M. Lipset, *op. cit.,* 3–53; Edward Shils, "The Intellectual in the Political Development of the New States," *World Politics* 12 (April 1970), 329–368. Lewis Feuer's *The Conflict of Generations* (New York: Basic Books, 1969) is a rich but strongly biased source of data on student movements. See also Richard Flacks, "Social and Cultural Meanings of Student Revolt," *Social Problems* 7 (Winter 1970), 340–357; and Richard Flacks, "Review Article: Feuer's *Conflict of Generations,*" *Journal of Social History* 4 (Winter 1970–71), 141–153.

2

GROWING UP CONFUSED: CULTURAL CRISIS AND INDIVIDUAL CHARACTER

It is not too great an oversimplification to say that the central, unifying theme of American culture has always been that cluster of values Max Weber called the "Protestant Ethic." In particular, Americans agreed that the meaning of life was given by one's work, that personal fulfillment and social responsibility required that males be fully engaged in a vocation, and that virtue was measured in terms of success in an occupation. The most valued work was entrepreneurial activity; the most valued model was the rational, thrifty, hard-working, self-denying, risk-taking entrepreneur.

Undoubtedly, the vitality of these values was important in the phenomenal growth of the American technological and economic system in the nineteenth century. In a period when accumulation and production were society's central problems, it was fortunate that the average man was highly motivated to produce, to work hard, and to save—in short, to resist temptations that might divert him from doing his part in building the country. It was also fortunate that aspirations for monetary success could be fulfilled by many, while many others could believe that their failure lay in themselves—in their own inability to achieve the cultural ideal—rather than in the ideal itself.

In the American ideal. women were not regarded as virtuous if *they* sought independence and success in the world of work. Instead, they were valued if they supported their husbands' capacity to be single-mindedly devoted to work, if they themselves were skilled at producing a self-sufficient household, and if they raised their male children to be independent, self-reliant, self-denying, and achievement-oriented individuals.

Given the entrepreneurial opportunities, the open frontier, and the evident dynamism of American life, it is not surprising that most American young people who were socialized into this cultural framework accepted it with enthusiasm. Boys were eager to become men in the image of their fathers—although encouraged by their fathers and mothers, they were profoundly eager to surpass their fathers' achievements in work and status.

Observers agree that this cultural framework has been severely eroded or at least modified by what has happened in America in the twentieth century. What, in brief outline, happened?

1. An economic system organized around problems of capital accumulation and the need for saving, entrepreneurship, and self-reliance—a system of free market and individual competition —has been replaced by an economic system organized around problems of distribution and the need for spending, interdependence, bureaucratic management, planning, and large-scale organization.

2. As a consequence, work is now coordinated by massive private and public bureaucratic organizations, and work achievement is defined not in entrepreneurial terms, but in terms of successful fulfillment of a career within a bureaucratic or professional hierarchy.

3. These developments have permitted and been required by a tremendous technological leap. Consequently, a vast array of commodities for individual consumption is produced. On the one hand, this situation required that men consume; on the other hand, it obviated the sense of the need to save, postpone gratification, and be self-denying that had been justified by scarcity.

As a result of these massive changes—from individual entrepreneurship to large corporate organization, from free market competition to bureaucratic coordination and planning, from accumulation and scarcity to consumption and affluence—the vitality of the "Protestant Ethic" has declined. Throughout society during the past sixty years, more and more people have felt less committed to the entrepreneurial character and its virtues. Increasingly, self-worth and worth in the eyes of others is organized as much by one's style of life and one's consumption patterns as by one's occupational status as such. Furthermore, although instrumental and rational activity is still highly valued, all observers report that there has been a relaxation on prohibitions against expressiveness and hedonism. Indeed, a society in which the consumption of goods has become a fundamental problem requires that men cease to be ascetic and self-denying and abandon many of the guilts that they experience when they express their impulses.

By the middle of the twentieth century, the American society was qualitatively different from the society that had given birth to the cultural framework of capitalism. The family firm had been superseded by the giant corporation, the free market by the "welfare-warfare" state, and the entrepreneur by the manager and the bureaucrat. Technology had created a superabundant economy in which the traditional virtues of thrift, self-denial and living by the sweat of one's brow seemed not only absurd, but actually dangerous to prosperity. Technology seemed to promise not only an abundance of goods, but a world in which hard physical labor could be eliminated.

Yet, despite the need for new values and a new cultural framework, a cultural transformation was not occurring. Politicians, teachers, and preachers continued to give lip-service to the Protestant Ethic, while the mass media, without announcing the fact, purveyed an increasingly blatant hedonism. Many of the classic symptoms of "anomie" were widespread. Breakdown was widely evident, but new values were not.

I suppose that the best indication of the coherence of a culture is the degree to which parents can transmit a sense of it to their offspring with clarity and effectiveness. Cultural breakdown has reached the point of no return when the process of socialization no longer provides the new generation with coherent reasons to be enthusiastic about becoming adult members of the society. Perhaps the best way I can illustrate what I mean by cultural instability and breakdown is to discuss the American middle-class family as it seemed to most observers to be functioning by mid-twentieth century. An examination of family patterns and child-rearing not only illuminates the cultural crisis, but also provides some clues to the sources of youthful discontent.

When you read what follows, remember that I am not criticizing American *parents* for faulty childrearing practices. On the contrary, the main point I am trying to make is that parental confusion is virtually inevitable in a society in which the culture is breaking down. Moreover, the outcomes of that confusion should not be labeled "pathological," in my opinion. On the contrary. When parents raise their children in a manner that causes them to have significant problems of "adjustment," if anything, this is a "healthy" circumstance. I am arguing that the basic source of socially patterned maladjustment is a culture that no longer enables a person to find coherent meaning in his life. The maladjustment of youth offers one of the few hopes that new meanings can be found—that a new culture can be created.

The family, of course, is the primary institution for the inculcation of basic values and molding of culturally appropriate character structures. All observers agree that the American family, particularly the white, "middle class" family, has undergone a substantial transformation over the past several decades—a transformation that both reflects and contributes to the cultural crisis in the society at large.

A major structural change in the middle class family has been its "reduction"—that is, the erosion of close ties to relatives outside the nuclear family unit. Dissolution of extended family bonds is highly functional in a society based on technological development because it permits people to be relatively free of emotional and economic ties to "homes" and "relatives" and enables them to move freely in response to changing occupational requirements, and to take advantage of opportunities for career advancement wherever and whenever they become available. Since the nuclear family is expected to establish a self-contained household, it becomes a highly efficient mechanism for absorbing a vast array of consumer goods—each small family unit seeks to purchase the house, car, furnishings, appliances, and other commodities that will ensure its independence. (On the other hand, an extended family complex living contiguously probably would share many such goods, thereby reducing the need for each household in the network to buy its own.) Thus, in a structural sense the nuclear middle class family meshes nicely with the economy's demand for a mobile labor force and an actively consuming public.

In the typical middle class family, the father works away from home while the mother spends virtually all her time at home rearing the children. Authority—in principle—is shared by the parents (a marked change from the patriarchal structure of the past), but clearly, it is exercised far more intensively and continuously by the mother than by the father. Ideally, the mother (if she is modern) is less concerned with efforts to repress and restrict the expressive, impulsive behavior of her children than she was in the past, just as she is less likely to emphasize obedient, submissive behavior as desirable. Instead, she is expected to facilitate the child's desires to explore, to test the environment, and to encourage self-reliant and autonomous behavior. What is now "good" is not so much the obedient, quiet, clean, cautious child, but rather the child who acquires verbal and motor skills early, who is precocious in his understanding, who can do things for himself, and who relates well to strangers and to other children. Mother attempts to instill such qualities by use of so-called "psychological" techniques of discipline—giving and withdrawing her love. She tries to avoid the traditional, more "physical" forms of punishment, trying instead to convey a nondomineering attitude, nurturing nonauthoritarian style. Father, relatively a part of the background, strives for a generally warm, nonauthoritarian and supportive approach.

This mode of childrearing has become ascendant in American culture in this century, especially in the last three decades. It relies, then, on a high degree of exclusive dependence on the mother coupled with strong demands on the child for cognitive mastery and a will to strive and achieve. Research suggests that this family situation is a superior one for generating precisely those characteristics that enable successful participation in a culture that stresses individual achievement, formal education, rationality, and flexibility. The culturally desired outcome of this family (and my emphasis here is on *male* character) is a child who achieves masculine identity and independence by fulfilling his mother's expectations that he will be independent and striving, whose guilt and anxiety is focused on achievement of internal standards of excellence, who enjoys testing and is capable of being tested, and who is able to handle sexual, aggressive, and other impulses and emotions by expressing them at the appropriate times and places while not letting them seriously interfere with his capacity for work, rational action, and self-reliance. Thus, impulses are not denied (as the traditional Protestant Ethic demanded) but managed. This process is greatly facilitated by the delicately balanced combination of demand and freedom, dependence and independence, and mothering and autonomy that ideally characterizes the suburban family.

How often such an "ideal" outcome actually results from this family situation is questionable. Although the mother-centered nuclear family meshes nicely with crucial *official values* embodied in the educational and occupational system, it appears to be highly vulnerable to a variety of severe contradictions that occur in the course of actual day-to-day life in the society. These contradictions are readily derivable from the general crisis of the culture I have been trying to sketch.

PARENTAL VALUE CONFLICT AND CONFUSION

Undoubtedly, parents experience a great deal of strain when they permit freedom and encourage autonomy on the part of their children. One source of such strain is the difference between the comparatively strict atmosphere in which most middle class parents were raised and the atmosphere they try to create in their own homes. Another is that many parents continue to be emotionally committed to the traditional virtues of cleanliness, obedience, emotional control, and the like. Undoubtedly, then, many mothers and fathers are quite inconsistent with respect to discipline and demands; sometimes they punish their children for infraction of their rules and at other times they do not; sometimes they insist on traditional "good habits" while sometimes they are more relaxed. Frequently such parental inconsistency may result in what has been called "absorption" of the child's personality. Rather than molding a flexible, striving, self-sufficient character, the result is a character who fears failure *and* success, experiences deep anxiety about his acceptance by others, finds it difficult to establish his own autonomy, and is, consequently, far more driven toward conformity and "security" than toward independence and personal achievement. Indeed, some social critics have argued that this "other-directed" character type is becoming ascendant and that the achievement-oriented, "inner-directed" type is fading. Whether or not this is true, it seems plain that parental confusion over the nature of discipline and virtue is widespread and seriously undermines cultural goals rooted in achievement motivation.

Many parents are clearly committed to providing opportunities for free expression and autonomy for their children. They favor a life of fulfillment, experiential richness, and less self-denial. They may desire such a life for *themselves,* but find it difficult to consistently and wholeheartedly treat their children in this manner. Clearly, parents in a small nuclear family revolving around the mother as the exclusive childcare specialist must expend a tremendous investment of patience and energy, especially if they exercise permissiveness. To permit children to wander, experiment, and test requires constant vigilance to protect their physical safety. To provide children intellectual stimulation and sensory variety requires intensive involvement in the quality of their activities. But if parents are to provide the quantities of time, energy, and patience required to achieve these goals they must limit their *own* recreation and pursuits and get enough sleep so that they will have sufficient energy and patience to allow their offspring to be the central focus of attention whenever the children are awake and around. Undoubtedly, this is a source of strain even for parents with articulate commitment to "liberated" values—perhaps especially for them, since they themselves want freedom, autonomy, and the like. This conflict between the demands of childrearing and the personal needs of the parents constitutes another source of parental inconsistency that undermines the "ideal" character of the modern middle class family.

A third source of parental confusion is the conflict between effort and indulgence. Typical middle class parents expect their offspring to strive and achieve and to understand the necessity for self-discipline and effort in attaining goals. Very often, however, such families have surplus incomes and try to provide their children with a sense of being well taken care of. Indeed, in many families, parents indulge their children in order to demonstrate their love and care. Many fathers assuage the guilt they feel because of their absence from the home by showering their children with presents; many rationalize their own self-sacrifice by averring that anything that frees their kids from suffering is worthwhile. In any case, such parental indulgence (which is undoubtedly functional for the consumer goods sector of the economy) tends to weaken the offsprings' sense of necessity for self-discipline, sacrifice, and toil. Indeed, many children of affluence sense that as heirs of their parents' material property, they are likely to have some degree of permanent lifelong economic security. Under these circumstances, effort and achievement lose much of their motivational potency and moral meaning. This is especially so if fathers suggest to their sons (which they often do) that they can afford to enjoy life in ways that previous generations could not.

Thus, it seems plausible that incoherence and confusion are virtually inevitable features of the modern middle class family and the suburban style of life. As we shall see, the consequences for the general culture and for the youths who will inherit it contribute to the sense of crisis.

MATERNAL AMBIVALENCE

In addition to such value confusion, there are other sources of childrearing imbalance and parental inconsistency. One of the most significant is the ambivalence and discontent that many women experience as they try to play the new maternal roles dictated by the family structure and childraising ideology we have been depicting. These discontents revolve around the fact that the woman who becomes a mother is expected to be a full-time mother and housewife in a situation in which she is highly isolated from adult social relations and must perform tasks that are menial and meaningless. She is expected to accept this role even though her formal educations before marriage and motherhood has made her qualified to perform other roles and despite her aspirations for independence and self-fulfillment. Understandably, such a woman finds it difficult to narrow her interests to the world of her three-year-old child and even more difficult not to feel guilty because she is discontent and hostile to her children and to her husband. The ways in which women have adapted to this situation are diverse. Most adaptations that have been recorded, however, have been condemned as culturally dysfunctional and/or psychologically damaging to the child. For instance, there is the smothering, over-protective mother (whose protectiveness is said to be a screen for her unconscious hostility toward the child). The "seductive" mother (who becomes extremely close to her son as a displacement for her more general interpersonal and sexual frustrations); the mother who subtly, and often unconsciously, denigrates her husband to her children as an expression of her jealous resentment of his privilege and his abandonment of her; the mother who attempts to live vicariously through her children (hoping that they will achieve goals that she herself has been blocked from achieving); and the working mother (who, according to some child-rearing experts, intensifies the child's fears of separation and abandonment).

All of these compensations are seen as damaging to the child's ability to manage and overcome his dependence on the mother, prolonging that dependency or forcing him to identify with her (instead of with the father) and weakening the male child's ability to accept culturally approved definitions of masculine identity. All of these patterns may weaken achievement motivation and damage the child's capacity for self-reliance.

Although many psychologists characterize such maternal behavior as "neurotic," a sociological perspective emphasizes the fact that such behavior is *socially determined—it is built into the maternal role* as it is now structured, especially considering the manner in which young women have been socialized and the increasing cultural support for the equality of women. More specifically, the discontent of middle class mothers is an inevitable consequence of the fact that they are forced into roles that do not match their aspirations and self-conceptions—aspirations and self-conceptions they have been taught are their right. Such a fundamental contradiction in women's roles is a further consequence and determinant of the general cultural crisis.

PATERNAL AMBIVALENCE

The paternal role contains its own built-in contradictions. This is so because fathers, as effective models of adult achievement, self-reliance, and rationality that they are expected to be, must be available for the psychological benefit of their children. At the same time, the middle class male who is striving or is already successful is likely to have a range of responsibilities and commitments outside the home. The highly career-oriented father may be available to his children hardly at all, partly from "necessity" and partly because he finds that life in the family is mundane when compared with life outside the home, where the responsibility and the power he can command are exciting.

Other fathers experience considerable regret and discontent with their work; they have ended up in positions that do not fulfill their earlier aspirations, they find their work unfulfilling or morally dubious, and they find work itself increasingly onerous. Many such fathers undoubtedly communicate their self-doubts and their skepticism to their sons. Still other men experience themselves as failures—as impotent and second rate in their work. The family, for them, becomes an arena for the exercise of power, aggression and self-importance which they cannot find elsewhere.

Like contradictions in the mothers' role, such paternal ambivalence is derived from fundamental cultural contradictions. These contradictions revolve around cultural demands for continuous striving and simultaneous demands for endless consumption—demands that men be dedicated careerists and, at the same time, good fathers, and that they compartmentalize the public and private worlds, reserving personal warmth, intimacy, and expressiveness for the latter.

A second source of strain for the middle class male is that the cultural measure of his worth (as well as his own sense of self-esteem) is based on his occupational success, but that success is a limitless goal on the one hand and is denied most men on the other. To the extent that the male accepts the cultural definition of his value, his self-esteem suffers. This inadequacy is communicated to his children; to the extent that he rejects the cultural standard, he communicates to his children a certain skepticism about the cultural framework.

As a result the developing child is exposed to another source of confusion. To the extent that the father embodies any of these contradictions, he is lacking in his effectiveness as a model, and since the typical suburban family is nuclear and isolated, the male child finds few alternatives to serve as effective models.

THE PACE OF SOCIAL CHANGE

A final source of parental confusion derives from the sense per-haps shared by most people in the culture—that the world in which children will be adults will be substantially different from the world in which they are children, in ways that are considerably obscure. Parents generally conceive of themselves—perhaps more than at any time in history—as inadequate models for their children because they are already obsolete. In this situation, the parental tone of voice lacks conviction, parental guidance has overtones of fatuousness, and parental authority is undermined by the parents' own lack of confidence. This particular source of cul-tural incoherence may not be directly related to the structure of the nuclear family itself, but it is a rather obvious consequence of a culture that values technological change and development as one of its central priorities. Presumably, a childrearing program that emphasizes independence, flexibility, and openmindedness meshes with a culture that values change. But as we have seen, such virtues are more easily espoused than instilled in a culture that places such heavy reliance on isolated and morally confused mothers and fathers to implement such a program.

It should not be hard to envision from our depiction of the built-in "strains" associated with the middle class nuclear family some idea of the consequences for young people. Briefly, such a family situation is likely to generate considerable confusion over values, goals, roles, and aspirations for the youth who experience it. More specifically, we can suggest that the "new" family is likely to impart a number of dispositions and personality "trends" in its offspring—traits or potentialities that predispose such youth to be restless with, skeptical of, or alienated from certain crucial aspects of conventional culture and, consequently, ready for certain kinds of cultural change.

A listing of some hypotheses concerning certain tendencies that the middle class family situation seems to generate in its offspring follows (I term them hypotheses, which await persuasive empirical tests, because for the most part, there is little direct evidence that these tendencies are clearly linked to childhood socialization):

1. Confusion and restlessness with conventional definitions of success. Such feelings would derive from the types of paternal ambivalence we have described, from the psychological distance of the father's work role from those of his sons', from the parental value confusions we have called attention to, and from the pattern of maternal domination. Even youths who have strong motivations to achieve and who may act these out in school would be likely to entertain doubts about whether material success, status-striving and careerism constitute appropriate avenues for expressing their desires to "do well." But neither conventional parents nor the conventional culture provide very many clues about how one can achieve in ways other than the economic. The consequences of this combination of predispositions to question material success coupled with predispositions to achieve include profound indecisiveness about vocation (what Erik Erikson has called "role confusion"), vague yearnings for recognition and fame, and a restless search for alternative vocations and life styles.

2. Restlessness under conditions of imposed discipline. These derive from such features of the family as parental indulgence and permissiveness and are related to feelings of discontent with conventional definitions of vocation and achievement. Some consequences are discontent with classroom drill and learning situations requiring rote memorization; tendencies to feel bored and restless when concentration is required; avoidance of school subjects requiring discipline and attention to detail; and a generalized resistance to tasks that do not appear to be personally rewarding or are set without reference to goals determined by the self. These feelings are accompanied by intense desires for immediate pleasure and release and immediate experience, often coupled with guilt.

3. Restlessness with conditions of arbitrary or coercive au-

thority. Such feelings might derive from expectations developed in the family for authority structures based on egalitarianism— expectations derived from parental fostering of participation, independence and autonomy and parental refusal to use physical punishment or coercion. Children raised in this way, we can speculate, may grow to expect that authority *outside* the family will be similarly responsive, democratic, nonpunitive and permissive. A consequence of such dispositions and expectations about authority is the tendency to be unusually trusting of teachers and other adults, but vociferously and unusually upset, angry and rebellious when such authority figures betray expectations that they will be egalitarian, democratic, and so forth. Or one might expect such children to be capable of more active expression of opposition and resistance to authority when it appears arbitrary, more skeptical of its claims in general, more likely to ask embarrassing questions, and more ready to systematically test the limits of its tolerance.

4. Discomfort with conventional sex-role definitions. Boys who have ambivalent fathers or who tend to identify with their mothers and have accepting, nonpunitive parents are likely to define masculinity in ways that are quite untraditional. They are likely to be less motivated for dominance, less physically aggressive and tough, less physically competitive, and more emotionally expressive and aesthetically inclined. Presumably, many girls raised in these ways are likely to be less submissive, more assertive, and more self-assured and independent. Insofar as parents continue to expect conventional sex-role performance on the part of their children—and insofar as such performance is expected by the schools and by peers—confusion and feelings of inadequacy can be the result.

Speculation on the kinds of traits, dispositions, and feelings that might be expected to be patterned outcomes of the family structure and childrearing practices we have been discussing could go on indefinitely, but the main line of our argument should be clear: certain major changes in social structure and economy have had a direct impact on the structure of the family, especially in the "middle class." These changes have also had a profound impact on the values and practices of parents. The result is a mixed one: on the one hand, the "new" family appears eminently suitable as an instrument for creating the "right" kinds of people for technological society; on the other hand, inherent in the same family situation are tendencies to generate profound feelings of dislocation and discontent with established values, institutions and roles. Thus, the American family, especially the middle class, suburban American family with its confusions and ambivalences, reflects the general crisis of American culture. At the same time, it contributes to that crisis by generating in the next generation aspirations, expectations, and impulses that are not compatible with established norms and institutionalized patterns. It creates the psychic grounds for new identities in a society that provides no models, roles, or life styles around which such new identities can crystallize.

The middle class family is *necessary* in advanced industrial capitalism. Nevertheless, it *necessarily* creates many youths who have trouble accepting the society. When the key institutions of socialization inherently generate tendencies toward nonconformity, there surely is a cultural crisis. This seems to be the situation that has developed in the United States during the last three decades, as families have had to come to grips with a cultural framework that no longer fits social reality.

Meanwhile, a similar pattern of incoherence is played out in all the other institutions responsible for socialization and cultural indoctrination. In the schools, the media and the churches, such contradictory values as self-denial and self-expression, discipline and indulgence, and striving and being are preached, dramatized, fostered, and practiced all at once. On the one hand, television and magazines advocate hedonism, consumption, and living it up, while schools and churches continue, uneasily, to embody the Protestant Ethic. The economy demands discipline and self-control in order to *make* a living and spending and self-indulgence as a *way* of living. Political leaders tend to espouse the old virtues, while pop culture celebrities systematically flout them. Incentives to strive, compete, and become disciplined are systematically undermined by affluence, but all institutionalized means to be creative and productive (as in high-level professional work) continue to be linked with demands to be competitive, striving and self-denying. An incredible number and variety of means are provided for hedonistic pursuit and sensuality, yet all such experience is heavily laden with guilt, is often defined as illegal or immoral, is prohibited to minors, or is so highly commercialized as to lose its authentically expressive character.

The incoherence of the general culture thus interacts with the confusion of the individual family. It seems probable that virtually all American youth experience cultural incoherence and "anomie" as an integral feature of their growing up. The argument we are making, however, would lead us to predict that the youth who experience this situation most acutely are those for whom conventional values have been most weakened or irrelevant. We shall return to this point.

BIBLIOGRAPHICAL NOTES

1. The "decline" of the "Protestant Ethic" has been discussed in many ways by many people. Weber's classic definition of the culture of capitalism appears, of course, in his *The Protestant Ethic and the Spirit of Capitalism* (New York: Scribner's, 1958). Joseph Schumpeter prophesied the decline of entrepreneurial values in *Capitalism, Socialism and Democracy* (New York: Harper, 1942). An influential work describing changes in the American character was David Riesman's *The Lonely Crowd* (New York: Doubleday-Anchor, 1953). Seymour Martin Lipset and Leo Lowenthal, *Culture and Social Character* (Glencoe, Ill.: Free Press, 1961) contains important commentary on Reisman's work, especially an essay by Talcott Parsons and Winston White.

2. My discussion of the American middle class family is heavily indebted to the following: Kenneth Keniston, *The Uncommitted* (New York: Harcourt, Brace & World, 1962); Riesman, *The Lonely Crowd*; A. W. Green, "The Middle Class Male Child and Neurosis," *American Sociological Review* 11 (1946): 31–41; Talcott Parsons and Robert F. Bales, *Family, Socialization and Interaction Process* (Glencoe, Ill.: Free Press, 1955); Daniel Miller and Guy Swanson, *The Changing American Parent* (New York: Wiley, 1958); Betty Friedan, *The Feminine Mystique* (New York: Norton, 1963); David C. McClelland, *The Achieving Society* (Princeton, N. J.: Van Nostrand, 1961); and Philip Slater, *The Pursuit of Loneliness* (Boston: Beacon, 1970). In addition, I have relied on impressions gathered from my research on families of activist and nonactivist students and from my own experience as a parent.

3

YOUTH: AN UNINTENDED CONSEQUENCE OF PLANNED CHANGE

Chapters 1 and 2 have been devoted to the argument that this society has undergone a major transformation of socioeconomic organization during the last half century—namely, the replacement of competitive, entrepreneurial capitalism by corporate capitalism. This transformation was paralleled by a massive growth in bureaucratic organization in both the private and public sectors, by a sharp increase in the importance of planning and coordinating economic and social life, by enormous advances in technological development, and by increased emphasis on consumption rather than on production.

I have suggested that one major consequence of this shift has been cultural incoherence—the fading vitality of those values and meanings that were relevant to entrepreneurial capitalism, the rising of new yearnings and motives, and a weakening of traditional means of social control. I have tried to show how this cultural incoherence particularly has affected young people because of the impact of cultural confusion on the family and other socializing institutions. And I have suggested that this situation makes many youths receptive to new values, meanings, and identities.

But anomie cannot by itself account for the rise of organized countercultures and oppositional movements. Processes that bring people together and facilitate interaction and mutual influence are equally important in the formation of collective action by masses of people. Those who face similar problems of adaptation, identity, and discontent but do not communicate because they are dispersed and unavailable to each other are likely to express and resolve their problems through a wide range of individual acts. Mass movements directed at social and cultural change require communication and resolution of a *common* consciousness; implementation of such processes is facilitated by geographic concentration.

As I have already suggested, American youth has indeed been experiencing concentration and segregation. The principal determinant of this process has been the rapid expansion of educational facilities, especially institutions of higher education. As I pointed out in Chapter 1, the existence of advanced educational institutions is the primary reason that youth exists as a stage of life and as a social category. As I suggested further, throughout history such institutions had been reserved for a small number of elite young men; only in the last few decades has such schooling been available to extensive masses of the young. The process of incorporating post-adolescent young persons into schools has greatly accelerated during the last decade. During the sixties, the number of youths in college doubled; by the beginning of the seventies a majority of high school graduates were entering college.

The rise of mass higher education is one of the most significant and dramatic changes in American society—if for no other reason than that it has created "youth" on a mass scale by segregating seventeen to twenty-one year olds in large numbers from other social groups and keeping them from full-time participation in the labor force. Effects of the higher education system, however, are considerably more far-reaching than that—as we shall shortly try to show.

The rise of mass higher education can be traced to the same socioeconomic transformations that have generated the cultural crisis:

First, the growth of corporate and public bureaucracy requires increased numbers of high level and middle level management personnel and many more persons with advanced technical and professional skills for the purposes of research, development, planning, coordination, social services, and the like.

Second, the commitment of industry and government to concerted, continuous, technological development requires massive increases in the number of scientists, engineers, and other technician to perform the research and development necessary to promote technological change. In the postwar period, such change has been concentrated heavily in the military sector but extends, of course, to other fields as well. For example, in recent years there has been rapid growth in all the services associated with medical and health care and a corresponding rise in the demand for a great variety of technical, professional, and service personnel.

Third, growth of the educational establishment itself requires new personnel at many levels. Indeed, the education "industry" has been one of the most rapidly expanding sectors of the economy because of technological change and because of the postwar "explosion" of the youth population. In addition, as educational achievement becomes increasingly defined as the major route to personal advancement, the grassroots demand for educational services becomes a further spur to expanding the "industry." Thus, the schools have grown in size to train more people to fill the jobs created by the growing school systems.

Fourth, increase in leisure time and uncommitted income creates demand for new types of recreation—both service and entertainment—and very often, the workers who perform these services need higher levels of education and training.

Fifth, the task of job training and retraining has shifted rather markedly from industry itself to the school system. Forms of vocational training previously carried out by individual corporations are now conducted by publicly funded high schools and community colleges.

Thus, the rapidly increased investment in higher education and the extension of it to the majority of young people was intended to meet a very central requirement of the economic system as it has been developing over the past five decades—the necessity for a massive upgrading of the labor force so that it could fulfill the demands of advanced technology and expanding bureaucratic organization. No longer was higher education to be restricted to the task of socializing the future governing class; it was now to produce a mass of people to do the advanced work of technological development and social management.

From the viewpoint of those policy-makers who fostered and planned the system of mass higher education, the objective was not simply to *train* a new class of educated workers, but to provide a mechanism for meritocratic selection for highly skilled occupational roles. Thus, the educational system was to become the primary route for upward mobility, the route that would enable millions of youths to achieve comfortable incomes and relatively high status even though their families had no real property.

Almost immediately, it became evident that this route was not available for most youths from working class and low income backgrounds who were being left out of the new university and college system. Nevertheless, these inequalities were concealed by the elaborate system of testing and selection that had developed—a system that had the appearance of rewarding the individual on the basis of qualification rather than privilege. Thus, one of the "functional" characteristics of mass higher education was to create at least the illusion that the society was according increasing equality of opportunity to young people regardless of their origins.

Undoubtedly, occupational opportunities for the college educated were opening up and a concomitant increment in lifetime earnings for those with college degrees would become available. No post-World War II observer who was witnessing the birth of mass university education actually doubted that these masses of college students would expend their energies in seizing these opportunities and in supporting the social order that had made them available.

In retrospect, however, we can see that such analyses of the functions of higher education and the expectations about the behavior of the college educated failed to see certain crucial dimensions of the schooling experience. Higher education inherently contains "functions" and generates consequences that are "latent," "unintended," and downright destabilizing from the viewpoint of those who wish it to serve as a productive resource for advanced technological capitalism.

However loudly humanists have lamented that liberal education is on the decline, a large proportion of students cannot escape exposure to a significant sampling of the cultural heritage —particularly to ideas and sentiments that are critical of the civilization, that propose cultural and social alternatives, and that provide tools for critical analysis of the social order. Indeed, the universities could hardly perform their manifest function of training managers, scientists, and intellectuals without providing training in rational criticism of the existing state of things. It is not surprising that some students take such ideas seriously and use them to interpret the world around them. For instance, some question racial inequality, nationalism, self-aggrandizement, commercialization of art, militarism, authoritarian methods of social control, the use of science for destructive purposes, political rhetoric and propaganda, institutional religion, and a variety of features of contemporary life that are regularly held up for scrutiny and criticism in the books they read, the courses they take, the lectures they attend, and the bull-sessions they stay awake for. Some students, particularly those in the hard sciences and technical fields, remain relatively immune to such experience because they become intensively specialized and overworked early in their college careers. But many do not—particularly those students who spend most of their time obtaining a general education—and thus the college experience "liberalizes" a very large proportion of students, at least to the degree that it prepares them to be receptive to social criticism. Furthermore, a fractional segment of students becomes active intellectuals—they choose to spend their lives as full-time critics, interpreters, and innovators of culture.

One of the consequences of educating students for critical analysis is that students tend to turn such analysis not only against the existing order as a whole, but against the university experience as such. The extent to which university authorities acted on the assumption that students were not adult and, hence, not entitled to adult rights with respect to either political expression or private affairs was an important aspect of university organization. This tradition of in loco parentis authority arose partly from the model of the elite college that was designed for the paternalistic nurture of the budding character of upper class young men—simultaneously protecting them from impersonal civil authority when they transgressed and providing them with appropriate moral guidance and restraint. More important, in loco parentis was rooted in the fear that officials of public institutions had of political reprisal for the "controversial" political or moral behavior of students. Many students who entered school in the late fifties and sixties had not only been raised by parents who were a good deal more tolerant and egalitarian than were the local deans, but also had acquired in their classes a considerable sensitivity to questions of civil liberty. Under these circumstances, it is not surprising that the traditional restrictions on student social life, its surveillance of dormitories, and its tendency to censor student publications, ban speakers, and outlaw organizations became an important focus of collective student concern and action almost as soon as the university opened its doors to mass education. One might say that the tradition of in loco parentis was a relatively trivial symbol of a more serious contradiction in the university experience—the peculiarly ambiguous situation of the student. Students were expected to be both adults and children at once; they were to be both independent and dependent, carefree and serious and autonomous and conforming. These were the norms and practices devised and institutionalized by universities of higher education, those institutions supposedly dedicated to rationality, coherence, and principle. Nothing was more likely to awaken the latent conviction of a considerable number of students that the society was fundamentally hypocritical.

However, the university experience had a second aspect: it provided a kind of freedom virtually unavailable elsewhere in the society. First, time was relatively free and unsupervised. The university student was at once free from the supervision of parents and the regimentation of work situations. His time was his own and he need not account for it to either his parents or his employer (as he would in a work situation).

Second, the student was expected to use some of his time to experiment with ideas, roles, life styles, and identities. The university years were regarded as a legitimate occasion for developing one's individuality and creativity. It was legitimate to stay up all night in intense philosophical conversation, to experiment with sex and establish intimate relations with members of the opposite sex, and to be open to unconventional ideas and practices rather than to organize one's time according to definitely goal-oriented production schedules. Thus, it is clear that one of the reasons university students all over the world can be mobilized for political action readily is because they have more surplus time and energy than do other members of society. Furthermore, students are permitted and expected to experiment with the new, avant-garde, dissenting elements in the culture.

Nevertheless, from the viewpoint of the official culture, the student is expected to strike an extremely delicate balance with respect to such freedom. In the immediate university situation, he is supposed to separate his free, searching, experimental role from his formal educational activity. With respect to academic activity, he is expected to be disciplined, rigorous, routinized, and submissive. Furthermore, he is expected to understand that student freedom is a special privilege that is restricted to those who were chosen for student status and restricted to the university years. From the perspective of the official culture, the student who would try to extend the freedom of university life to people outside the university or maintain it for himself upon leaving the university setting would be making a serious error.

Such a balance might be preserved if students had vocational clarity (and were willing to subordinate themselves to the rigors of the curriculum), and if they perceived the culture as coherent and their own privileged place in it as clear and valid. Apparently, the balance between conformity and rebellion in the university is lost in an atmosphere of cultural breakdown and identity crisis. Students come to question the disciplines of the curriculum insofar as they demand self-regimentation because these disciplines assume the viability of a culture that has become obsolete in their eyes. Students come to feel that they are being trained for vocations that are either nonexistent or irrelevant to their aspirations. Eventually, they wish that the freedom of student life could be prolonged indefinitely: why should life not be devoted to self-development? Why confine development of one's imagination, creativity, values, and life styles to a few years of one's youth—restricted even then by arbitrary authority imposed by an outmoded hierarchy? Furthermore, isn't it immoral that this freedom should be available only to a small number of privileged youths? What gives *us* the right to such luxurious freedom while the rest of the world is bound by grinding economic necessity to hard labor, regimented work, and burdensome responsibility?

On the American scene, such questions were reinforced by two relatively unique features of the student situation. First, the privileged status of students was enhanced by student deferments from conscription—a situation that heightened both the wish to prolong student status and the guilt associated with having that status. Second, the material abundance and technological capacity of the society made even more glaring the irrationality of student freedom, for society seemed to have the capacity to grant similar opportunities for growth and individual expression to millions of nonstudent youths who were forced into the military, left in urban ghettoes, or locked into marginal jobs.

In any case, the point I am trying to make is this: the university provided certain kinds of freedom for students—enough freedom so that many were able to act out their discontents rather easily. This taste of freedom only served to heighten the yearning for its extension. Many students imagined a *life* based on such freedom; others questioned the legitimacy of their own privileges. In this sense, many students took university life too seriously. They were supposed to interpret its free-thinking, unregimented, expressive, communal qualities as an experience to be tasted and then abandoned. They were expected to understand that the right to participate in such a life as adults was reserved for a small number of persons willing to commit themselves to the rigors and self-limitations of scholarship.

Some of them did not "understand." Instead, their hope for more universal attainment of such a life assumed a reality that was not compatible with a culture suitable to industrial capitalism.

In addition to arousing in individual students both intellectual and emotional bases for social criticism and cultural opposition, university life, as we have already implied, united masses of students who had such emerging sentiments. Probably never in human history has a society brought together such a large number of potential dissidents in such large aggregates and under conditions that so greatly facilitated their mutual influence.

Marx averred that aggregation of the industrial proletariat in the factory was one element that enabled the working class to develop a class consciousness. Because they were united in a common work situation, they were able to communicate their discontents to each other and develop a common perspective. Even Marx did not envision institutions in which ten, twenty, thirty, or forty thousand persons who worked side by side would live together in common communities and under conditions that afforded considerable free time for intensive communication.

In retrospect, it is hard to doubt that the emergence of a collective consciousness among students—student culture—was inevitable. Moreover, the fact that so many students entered this environment with a certain disposition to "alienation" and found this alienation reinforced by the curriculum and the extracurriculum increased the likelihood that this consciousness would be not only distinct from the general culture, but in some discord with it.

Students were not the only sector of the youth population that was being segregated and concentrated during the fifties and sixties. First, in this period, a standing army of at least 3 million young men was developed. One latent function of the military—especially when it is based on conscription—is to segregate a large mass of discontented youths from the general populace and permit it to interact and develop a common consciousness.

Second, technological changes that led to the necessity for a massive upgrading of the labor force (and to a system of higher education for the masses) also led to the exclusion from the labor force of hundreds of thousands of poor youths who could not participate in the educational system because of the systematic downgrading of the schools they had attended. Many of these youths were drafted, but a high proportion could not meet the physical and mental requirements of the Selective Service system. Since these unemployed or marginally employed youths were segregated and concentrated in the urban ghettoes they were easily able to develop a distinct "subculture" and movement of social opposition.

Thus, the rise of mass university education, the growth of a conscripted army, and the burgeoning of the urban ghetto created crucial conditions for the emergence of youth as a distinct social category during the last two decades. All of these institutional transformations were associated with the postponement of adulthood—that is, the exclusion of physically mature young people from full-time participation in the labor force. All of these changes led to the concentration of youth in separate enclaves—a concentration that fostered a growth of collective awareness and a sense of, distinctiveness. All of these transformations intensified the dissatisfaction of those who were affected by them, thus creating the motivational basis for collective movements of opposition within these enclaves.

Undoubtedly, these institutional developments were not the only factors that promoted the sense of distinctiveness and collective consciousness among young people. Alongside the physical aggregation of youth technology was operating to enhance and generalize the idea of youth as a separate social type. I am referring, of course, to the rise of the mass media—the introduction, in the lifetime of today's youth of the following communications innovations: television, long playing records, tape recordings, hi-fi and stereo radio and phonograph equipment, FM radio, and paperback books. Development of these innovations was in addition to the continuing development of slightly older inventions: films, AM radio, and the mass-circulation weekly, for example. As everyone knows, post-World War II youth has been raised with an unprecedented degree of involvement with these media. Such involvement is stimulated and exploited by the media industries and by their advertisers, who wish to tap a vast market; young people collectively, despite their exclusion from the labor force, have billions of uncommitted dollars at their disposal.

In the United States, youth subcultures have been manifest for a number of decades. Until recently, however, youth was segmented into a variety of diverse and often hostile subcultures. Slum youth tended toward various "delinquent" subcultures. Middle class white high school youth tended to adopt a way of life that revolved around sports, dating, and "fun." In the colleges, a polarization had existed for several decades between "collegiate" students (who were oriented toward fraternities and intercollegiate athletics and against academic pursuits) and "intellectual" students (who stressed unconventional life styles and a commitment to intellectual and aesthetic activity). Alongside these were many local variants. Meanwhile, the majority of young people were not aware of themselves as members of any distinct, age-defined category.

One impact of the mass media has been to homogenize the content of the youth culture. Increasingly, today's youth of all strata, regions, and situations tends to orient to the same music, dress fashion, symbols, jargon, and general ambience. It can be argued that in many respects the new youth culture is a *creation* of the mass media and consumer goods industries, which have a commercial interest in exploiting a mass youth market ready to purchase the materials necessary for acceptance as a bona fide participant in the subculture. The new music would be unthinkable without stereo records and tapes; TV and the magazines calculatingly spread particular life styles by broadcasting stereotyped versions of these for all youth to experience.

Virtually every element of the emerging youth culture—new tastes in clothes, in music, in literature, in film, in arts and crafts, in modes of transportation, and so on—could and did become a marketable item. The language, symbols, and imagery of youth culture were incorporated into advertising and popular entertainment formats. Magazines and newspapers assigned specialists to monitor the changing tastes of the young, while new periodicals emerged to reflect and shape these tastes. In fact, the emergent tastes and symbols were so systematically exploited by commercial interests that it was virtually impossible to separate the manipulated from the spontaneous. Was a rock group popular because it authentically reflected the moods of its audience or because media men decided that it was popular and promoted it?

In this book, I tend to take the position that crucial elements of the youth culture that developed during the sixties were authentic expressions of young artists and cultural innovators. Such elements could not have been created on the drawing boards of Madison Avenue and Tin Pan Alley; in fact, they were created in precise opposition to the commercialization of culture. One of the central ironies of our time, however, is that expressions of cultural opposition can become means to lucrative commercial exploitation. As we shall see, the paradox goes even deeper—for the marketing of the unconventional by the mass media did not simply co-opt cultural alienation; it helped to spread it and strengthen its impact on masses of youth.

But I am getting ahead of my story.

BIBLIOGRAPHICAL NOTES

1. The rise of mass higher education is analyzed in, Christopher Jencks and David Riesman, *The Academic Revolution* (Garden City, N. Y.: Doubleday, 1968).

2. "Strains" in American higher education that were evident in the years prior to the emergence of mass protest are discussed in R. Nevitt Sanford (ed.), *The American College* (New York: Wiley, 1962).

3. The analogy between students and factory workers is developed by a number of writers. See, for example, Rowntree and Rowntree, "Youth as Class," *Our Generation* 6 (1968): 155–90; I. L. Horowitz and W. Friedland, *The Knowledge Factory* (Chicago: Aldine, 1970), Chapter 5, "Students as a Social Class"; and H. Gintis, "The New Working Class and Revolutionary Youth," *Socialist Revolution* 1 (May–June 1970): 13–44.

4

YOUTH AS AN AGENCY OF CHANGE: THE COUNTERCULTURE AND THE MOVEMENT

Our argument so far has been this: We take seriously the rise especially during the last ten years of a counterculture based in youth and of mass movements of political opposition also based in youth. We observed that such generational revolts have occurred in other historical times and places and have typically been symptomatic of major social and cultural transformations. Nevertheless, until the last decade, generational revolt has been virtually absent in American society. We wondered whether any major structural changes that could cause a major sociocultural crisis had occurred. We suggested that fundamental transformations in the political economy associated with dominance of the giant corporation associated with the state and with the rise of advanced technology were having profound disintegrative effects on the culture. These effects were particularly noticeable in the family—especially in connection with raising children—were reflected in a general cultural incoherence, and were producing an increasing number of young people who were experiencing identity crises. Either their character structures (motives, impulses, values, and aspirations) were considerably at variance with the established institutional framework or they were fundamentally dislocated and restless because of the intensifying anomie that they were experiencing.

These structural transformations produced not only culture and identity crises, but also an institutional framework in which youth inevitably became a definite social category. Mass higher education, the conscripted army, and the urban ghetto were social developments that entailed postponement of adulthood for millions of persons. Simultaneously, these institutions were enclaves within which the discontented young were gathered together, thereby facilitating the development of collective consciousness and action. In themselves, these enclaves were institutions that profoundly reinforced and intensified the grievances, discontents, and alienations of many of those within them. Finally, technology applied to communications provided the structural basis for the interlinking of local enclaves and the emergence of an increasingly homogeneous consciousness among youth throughout the American society and even internationally.

Mass consciousness does not emerge overnight. Neither is it unanimous by any means. If we were to stop our analysis with the argument as it has so far been presented, we would find it very hard to account for the following facts:

Both the youth counterculture and the new left began as decidedly minority expressions and, initially, were reactions against the values and styles that then prevailed among the young.

Both the counterculture and the movement were originated by a very particular, and rather unrepresentative, sector of the youth population as a whole.

The youth population remains internally differentiated and exhibits a rather wide range of behaviors. Even now, a considerable number of persons do not seem "youth"-ful. The movements in question have themselves changed markedly over the past decade. They have grown numerically; they have become increasingly polarized from the conventional and the established and increasingly hostile to authority. On the other hand, during the early seventies, many of the forms and styles that developed during the sixties seemed themselves to be disintegrating.

Having sketched the broad social and cultural trends that have had an impact on young people, we must now examine youths' efforts to respond to those trends. As we shall see, what happened in the sixties was not simply a mass reaction of youth to a set of objective circumstances. It was also an outcome of initiatives taken by certain groups of young people—initiatives designed to overcome the social and personal crises that these youths encountered. If our argument so far has emphasized the fact that youth has been *made by* history, we now shift our emphasis to regard youth as *making* history.

THE "FUNCTION" OF YOUTH CULTURE

It is important to realize that whenever "youth" exists as a stage of life, a "youth culture" is likely to arise. It is also important to stress that such a development may be quite functional both for individual development and for the stability of complex societies. Indeed, until the sixties, sociologists usually argued that youth culture *supported* the conventional American value system. Their argument was something like the following:

Speaking in broad terms, we can say that in traditional society, the establishment of adult identity is not problematical. Who one is is determined very largely by one's cultural, social, and geographical locations at birth. Parents, grandparents, and other elders not only transmit the accumulated past of one's culture, but also represent the way to become and be adult.

In "modern"—industrial, urban—society, identity formation is very much a problem. The vocations, practices, and beliefs of parents and grandparents are made substantially irrelevant by the pace of change. The social need for a highly mobile, flexible, and specialized work force means that socialization for adulthood will be carried out not by one's older kin, but by a professionalized set of educators, in settings that require intense mingling with many strangers. Migration, travel, and advanced means of communication flood young people with cultural influences of every conceivable variety. Given the uncertainty of societal and personal future, the absence of closeup models of viable maturity, and the necessary impersonality of the formal socialization process, young people in advanced societies characteristically look to each other for mutual assistance in making the transition to adulthood. In this sense peer cultures are substitutes for the traditional family:

they provide interpersonal support and intimacy for youths who are adapting to adult roles involving responsibility and independence.

In addition, adolescent peer cultures are agencies of socialization. In particular, they enable young people to acquire experiences and skills that schools and other official institutions ignore and for which families are inadequate and irrelevant. For example, participation in a peer culture provides a variety of ways in which its members can test and develop their competence in informal social relations. They are the primary medium for developing sexual competence and identity—the most salient institution for developing the sense of what it means to be adequately male and female and the degree to which one can meet conventional social standards in this regard. Beyond this, however, youth cultures tend to embody a complex of orientations toward adult culture in general and toward school in particular. Since sense of self is highly dependent on the treatment one receives from his peers and because adolescent identity is precarious, youth cultures are very effective in enforcing their standards through the process of allocating status within them. Young people who cannot or will not conform to the expectations or accept the orientations of the surrounding peer culture are likely to be isolated and excluded— an experience that can be extremely painful and disorienting.

If each young person had to face the problem of adult identity as an individual, each would experience profound confusion and anxiety (although society would be composed of persons who were either highly individuated—and perhaps creative—or broken and paralyzed). To the degree that the youth culture's orientations and expectations about sex roles and other basic values are *continuous* with the orientations, standards, and values of the prevailing culture, each individual who can accept and be accepted by the youth culture experiences relatively minor problems of identity. Problems of identity, then, are especially acute for those who do not attain such acceptance. These people are either isolated and withdrawn or they participate in deviant or unconventional peer cultures. Clearly, problems of self-esteem and clarity are greatest for those in solitary isolation; deviant subcultures provide at least confidence and within-group status even if they do intensify the tensions between the individual participant and the larger culture.

Sometimes, however, deviant youths can influence the majority. Many years ago, Karl Mannheim observed that generational movements have their beginnings in what he called "generational units." When small groups of young people form around a particular set of new perspectives and begin to establish a distinct and visible cultural pattern in opposition to those that are established, they may (or may not) capture the interest of widening circles of individuals in their own age groups. Movements of generational opposition, then, do not arise all at once; instead, small group of peers act as a vanguard to such movements.

I believe that Mannheim's concept of generational units is crucial to understanding the transformation that occurred in American youth culture. Clearly, as I suggested in the Introduction, the youth culture that prevailed in American high schools and colleges prior to the sixties was smoothly integrated with the most conventional values and sentiments held by American adults. Something that happened in the late fifties and early sixties changed this situation; that something, I want to argue, was the emergence of a new generational unit—a subculture of youth that looked at first like a deviant group but turned out to be a vanguard.

What did youth culture look like in the fifties? Dimensions of the high school culture that prevailed then included the following: rigid definition of sex role behavior (boys were expected to be athletic, cleancut and crewcut, antiintellectual and antiacademic, sexually exploitative, and callous; girls were expected to be well-groomed, to play down their intellectual capabilities, and to be date-conscious and "social," mushily romantic over popular "crooners," and frivolous and marriage-oriented. Teenage activity was organized and supervised by adults through school sports, dances, and the like; pop music was created, manufactured, and distributed according to formulas and tastes established by adults. Political interest and activity was "out." Defiance of adult authority existed, but it was expressed largely through overt disdain for academic achievement (though obviously many were covertly conforming in order to get to college) and through experiments with *adult* hedonistic prerogatives—getting drunk, driving fast, smoking, petting. Obviously, overcommitment to this peer culture could be damaging to the achievement of maturity (the story of the aging high school football hero who fails as a man was a cliche movie plot in the fifties). Nevertheless, assimilation into this culture was the obvious way of establishing a conventionally grounded identity and capacity for "normal" social and sexual roles.

Similarly, observers of the college campus scene during the fifties were universal in their reports that the student body was disturbingly "conformist," "complacent," "politically apathetic," and "privatized." Apparently, college students emulated the primary concern of their middle class adult counterparts—concern with their own material security, with the status race, and with bland forms of conventional fun.

To be sure, a large number of boys and girls could not be assimilated by the middle class youth culture. Typically, these were working and lower class youth and members of ethnic and racial minority groups who had been rejected by the school systems and deprived of an opportunity to attain occupational mobility. Such youths adapted to their exclusion by the system and by other youths of their own age by forming "delinquent" subcultures— groups that symbolically and behaviorally expressed defiance of school and community authority, carried on self-organized social life in the streets, and, in some cases, engaged in organized truancy, petty theft, vandalism, and violence.

There was also a fraction of middle class youth that felt excluded from and repelled by the prevailing youth culture. These were typically young people who were academically motivated and successful, who had internalized middle class norms of citizenship, and who were repelled by delinquency, violence, and aggression. Yet, they were equally (or even more) repelled by the frivolity, antiintellectualism, and social indifference of the middle class peer culture and by its stereotyped sex role definitions and superficial conventionalism. These were boys who were intellectual and aesthetic rather than athletic and aggressive, and girls who were "brainy" and assertive and consciously antagonistic to conventional femininity—young people who were uneasy in the conventional round of dating, disdained careful grooming, and wanted to be serious and individualistic. As a result, their status within the prevailing youth culture tended to be low, and they were likely to suffer from anxiety and self-doubt that such lack of acceptance usually entails.

Where did such apparently "deviant" middle class youth come from? In retrospect, we can see clearly that they represented an important new social type in American culture—they were the offspring of a definite and increasingly established stratum of the American middle class. At the time, however, many perceived themselves to be freaks of nature, mysteriously unable to wholeheartedly embrace what was apparently "normal."

I call such young people "intellectual youth" in part because the identities they sought to establish were intellectual. They were concerned with basic questions of value, with books and the arts, and with critical examination of basic assumptions of culture. They were "intellectual" in the related sense that they identified with that aspect of American and western civilization that was antimaterialistic, and antibourgeoisic—cultural values upheld by many of the artists, writers, poets, and intellectuals of the nineteenth and twentieth centuries.

In earlier eras intellectual youths were likely to be isolated individuals alienated from the mainstream of youth and intensely estranged and lonely in relation to their peers. Such estrangement caused considerable anxiety and unhappiness, but in some fortunate cases strong positive impulses toward introspection, nonconformity, and creativity also resulted. Bookish youths constructed their identities less on the basis of their immediate social relations than on the basis of the literature and art of similarly alienated intellectuals of previous generations.

No doubt this pattern of individuation continues to this day. Toward the end of the fifties, however, a new situation was evident —the emergence of a *critical mass of alienated intellectual youth.* The search for cultural alternatives had become a collective enterprise rather than primarily an individual one. Increasingly, young intellectuals were able to find each other and work out the beginning of a style of being youthful that represented a coherent alternative to the conventional peer cultures from which they had been excluded. By the end of the fifties, their impulses and interests, their tastes and perspectives, and their appearance and demeanor had, for many, ceased to be sources of embarrassment, shame, and worry and had begun to be matters of pride and self-esteem.

If a considerable increase in the number of intellectual youths made possible the emergence of an intellectual subculture among them, it is important to understand how and why this increase occurred. Intellectual youths are usually offspring of parents who are engaged in intellectual vocations—doctors, lawyers, teachers, scientists, administrators, and professionals in the social services and communications, for example. This category, which is composed of vocations that require a college education, was one of the labor force sectors that had been most rapidly expanding during the previous three decades. Thus, the increase in the number of intellectual youths during the fifties and sixties is directly traceable to the fact that the proportion of parents of adolescents who had attended college, developed intellectual, aesthetic, and "humanistic" orientations, and been engaged in intellectual and professional occupations had increased.

In Chapter 3, I enumerated a number of unintended consequences of mass higher education. Here, then, is another: mass higher education produces some parents who raise their children to want to be "intellectuals."

Research has found that there is a cluster of values and child-raising attitudes and practices that is characteristic of this occupational group (obviously, it is not universal for or exclusive to this group). This cluster of values, interests, attitudes, and practices is particularly characteristic for families in which the *mother* is college educated and career-oriented. It has taken root especially in the largest cities, especially among secularized Jewish and Protestant families.

With respect to *values,* these families emphasized the primary importance of commitment to the world of ideas and the arts rather than to personal material success or religious devotion. One might say that for them, the university, rather than the church or the business concern, has been the primary institutional repository of value and virtue. Furthermore, they tend to be humanitarian in ideological terms—to stress the value of being socially useful in one's work and of taking the role of citizen seriously. With respect to leisure and recreation, these families tend to emphasize pursuits that will promote culture—reading good literature, listening to music, visiting museums, and traveling for cultural enrichment are preferred over spectator sports or escapist recreation. Education is highly valued less for its instrumental value than for its intrinsic merits. Members of this group are politically informed and generally quite liberal, although only a minority are politically active.

Since both parents in these families are highly educated and, often, both are involved in careers or full-time occupations, a relatively high degree of equality between the parents is maintained. Household responsibilities are shared, as are family decisions; these are not families in which the father is the dominant authority or the mother is the controlling figure in day-to-day child care—especially if the mother is working. Typically, family egalitarianism extends to the children as well; the parents espouse support for the autonomy and free expression of their children and often encourage or expect independence and self-expression. Physical punishment is rare, and the parents typically adopt a relaxed attitude in regard to certain traditional middle class areas of rigid parental concern—cleanliness, toilet training, impulsiveness, sexual play, and general obedience, for example. Nevertheless, these parents are *not* permissive with respect to those aspects that are central to their lives; they have high expectations for their children with respect to intellectual achievement, and they expect their offspring to be verbal, interested in books, creative, and talented artistically. These parents are likely to exercise active control over the expression of aggression—actively discouraging hostile and "selfish" behavior while encouraging cooperative and gentle behavior. It should be added that ideally, this combination of encouragement of autonomy, control over aggression, and expectation for intellectual achievement is made coherent by the overall value system expressed, and occasionally lived, by the parents.

Perhaps you can see that these families, as I have described them, are less prone than most to some of the frustration, ambivalence, and incoherence that I identified as characteristic of the contemporary middle class family. To a considerable extent, these parents are likely to be *more consistent and principled* than are most parents: this appeared to be true of many families I studied in Chicago and of the families described by Kenneth Keniston in his study of radical youth. Particularly clear was that these parents desired to impart to their offspring a commitment to intellectualism and a critical attitude to prevailing cultural goals—particularly with respect to materialism, conventional morality, status seeking, and mass culture. Clearly, they wanted their children to be academically serious, involved with the arts and books, and oriented toward intellectual careers and social responsibility.

On the other hand, many such parents were likely to express either overtly or covertly some ambivalence about their own lives. They were people who had achieved a considerable degree of material well-being, but were likely to feel some guilt about their own comfort and privatism in a world in which poverty and gross inequality prevailed. They were likely, by the time their kids were adolescents, to have experienced some disillusionment about the degree to which their vocations were personally rewarding and socially useful or to which society was moving in the political, social, and cultural directions they had hoped for in *their* youth. Although they hoped their children would maintain or enhance their social status through fulfilling and useful occupational attainments, they also tended to stress the necessity of living in accordance with one's values more consistently than they themselves had done.

Thus, by the late fifties, young people who had been infused with critical attitudes toward the culture and endowed with character traits that set them apart from more conventionally raised peers thronged the schools and colleges. Because of their values, interests, and character structures, many of these people felt excluded and repelled by the prevailing youth culture.

These were the youths, then, who formed the nucleus of an *alternative* subculture on certain large university campuses during the late fifties—one within which their own values and aspirations could be freely expressed and social acceptance could be achieved.

What attitudes did the intellectual campus subculture express during the late fifties? First, an increasingly overt rejection of the symbols and practices of the prevailing youth culture. Campus nonconformists replaced "good, clean grooming" with casual dress and bearded faces, girls let their hair down and wore little or no makeup, sandals replaced white bucks, and jeans and sweatshirts replaced ivy league attire. Intellectuals preferred modern jazz and folk music to popular, commercial "tin pan alley" music, and many of them took up the guitar and other folk instruments and performed in or frequented the newly sprouting coffee houses in campus neighborhoods. The young intellectuals sought "intimate" friendships and love relations rather than superficial sociability and the dating ritual. The content of social relationships was defined less by frivolity and gossip than by "serious" intellectual discussions about philosophy, politics, culture, and religion. Friendship, art, ideas, and experience were highly preferred to commercialized entertainment, organized athletics and spectator sports, school spirit, and other conventional uses of leisure time.

Above all, the intellectual subculture expressed a romantic identification with the life styles of bohemian artists and with rather sanitized versions of folk culture, especially American Negro culture. A powerful influence by the end of the fifties were the beat generation poets and writers whose stance of bohemian opposition to American culture was vividly publicized. Most participants at the time probably did not conceive of being bohemian as a possible vocation; instead many hoped that academic careers would give them the personal freedom and intellectual stimulation necessary to avoid the "rat race." Undoubtedly, many were attracted to the "hipster" apotheosized by Norman Mailer: a man who could reap the material benefits of a conventional career while cultivating a *psychological* disaffiliation from it, exploiting organized society while living psychically apart from it. Thus, initially, the mood of campus intellectuals was one of alienation from prevailing culture, especially the culture of their peers. On the other hand, it shared with that culture a rejection of collective action and public protest, although a minority of participants maintained an interest in the tiny radical and socialist sects and clubs that continued to survive on a number of the big campuses.

Thus, the emergent intellectual subculture expressed, explicitly and implicitly, alienation from middle class conformity and conventionality; superficial social relations and role playing; conventional definitions of "success" based on money, consumership, and careerism; and the trivial, commercial, and inauthentic character of pop culture. For its adherents, creativity, individuality, personal authenticity, intellectual seriousness, and cultivated cultural tastes and preferences were the highest personal virtues. And it expressed aspirations for the attainment of a genuinely individual identity and for the discovery of ways of being adult that would enable such identities to fully realize their potentialities.

Even in its earliest beginnings, participation in the emergent subculture was not restricted to youth who had been explicitly socialized with these sentiments—although we are arguing that such youth were the primary element in its creation. Nevertheless, it is crucial to recognize that in addition to the sons and daughters of the "intelligentsia," substantial numbers of other upper middle class young people were finding the conventional youth culture inadequate for resolving problems of identity.

Of particular relevance in this regard is Kenneth Keniston's depiction of "uncommitted" youth. In the course of conducting a study at Harvard University during the late fifties, Keniston discovered a small group of undergraduates who were highly estranged from their peers and had profoundly rejected American culture. As he describes them, these students had not been reared in the coherent, liberal, humanist style that we have attributed to "intellectual" families. Instead, Keniston's family type was composed of the following elements: a father who was substantially inadequate as a model for his son either because of actual physical absence, psychological distance, or personal inadequacy; a mother who was considerably ambitious, talented, or artistic but who was unlike the typical intellectual mother in that she was trying to satisfy her extremely frustrated ambitions through her son's achievements. This combination of parents, according to Keniston, caused a situation in which the son identified with the mother, adopting many of her interests and aspirations, and was likely to have been protected, indulged, and psychologically seduced by the mother. Moreover, neither parent was likely to possess or communicate to their children any coherent value system or personal direction. Such young men, Keniston argues, had major problems in achieving independence and profound difficulties in relating or conforming to conventional definitions of masculine sex roles. In short and in an extreme form, Keniston's subjects represent one outcome of the confused middle class family described in Chapter 2. Very likely, some young men of this type found the emergent intellectual youth culture attractive because it offered avenues of expression and recognition that were denied by the conventional youth culture and the school system.

As we have described them, intellectual and "uncommitted" youth shared a sense of revulsion with and exclusion from the collective life of their peers. They shared impulses and interests that made them diverge from standardized sex role definitions.

Both types were considerably uneasy about entering the occupational world for which school was preparing them. Both sought interpersonal depth, experiential richness, and moral seriousness —dimensions they found absent in the social life of their peers and in conventional adult society as well. Both sought new bases for identity that would permit these impulses and aspirations to be realized.

The fundamental difference between the two types rests on the fact that the "intellectuals" had some coherent value system provided by their parents to sustain and orient them while in the pure case, the "uncommitted" were more confused and adrift and, therefore, more passive and present-oriented.

On the surface, formation of a subculture of alienated, intellectual youth may be interpreted as an inevitable and functional development. Given the growth of a highly educated segment of the labor force, dissatisfaction of a large number of youths who had been born into this stratum with the conventional youth culture was inevitable. Since peer cultures appear to be an essential ground for identity formation in advanced industrial society, it was to be expected that youths from this stratum, once they had become sufficiently numerous to do so, would create a differentiated subculture more in accord with their motivational and character structures. From the perspective of functional analysis, one could argue that such differentiation enables such youth to develop more easily the identity structure and interpersonal competences appropriate to intellectual and professionalized careers —to grow up in the relatively highly individuated fashion necessary for certain elite roles in established society. This analysis would predict, then, that young people would be relatively stably stratified, with a variety of youth subcultures coexisting and, in a sense, channeling youth into the various strata of preexisting adult society. Indeed, one would expect youth cultures to be *alternatives* to overt rebellion, as long as they are adequately tolerated and legitimized by adult authorities. The energy of alienated intellectual youth, once institutionalized in a distinctive subculture, would serve the functional requirements of the going system.

But the subculture of young intellectuals did not remain deviant. Nor did its members become less rebellious as they found means to social acceptance. On the contrary, this apparently deviant subculture came to influence and attract the apparently conventional majority of the young. Moreover, over the course of the subsequent decade the initially mild cultural criticism articulated by young intellectuals became increasingly political, radical, and rebellious.

How did the intellectual youth subculture *diffuse* beyond the ranks of its initial participants? In a society with very little precedent for radical political movements among its youth, how did a mass movement with revolutionary overtones come into being? These are the problems I want to look at next.

DIFFUSION OF THE "INTELLECTUAL" YOUTH CULTURE

As I have suggested, youth culture appears to be a functional requisite of advanced industrial society as a medium for identity formation and preparation for adulthood. That the prevailing youth culture of postwar America could not encompass the needs of certain types of high status youth was not particularly surprising, nor was it unusual that these youths should band together to form a counterculture that provided the basis for a more individuated, intellectual, and critical identity. Particularly surprising is the fact that this counterculture did not remain (as "deviant" subcultures usually do) a restricted enclave for the marginal few, but became the dominant subculture on many campuses and in many regions of the country and a significant force in all locations where youth were aggregated.

In interpreting processes of diffusion, it is very important to strive for some precision in specifying the manner in which various discrete cultural elements diffuse. Clearly the "alienated" youth culture did not constitute a single, seamless entity, and in our discussion thus far no doubt we have been guilty of treating "it" as a thing. Instead, we are talking about a cluster of interrelated but separable elements: art forms, fashions, jargon, behavior patterns, values, and norms. We are also talking about social circles, friendship groups, and acquaintance networks. Thus, "participation" in a subculture is a convenient but oversimplified way of talking about a very diverse number of ways in which persons may orient to the cultural and social syndrome we are describing. They may accept some cultural elements, while being ignorant of, indifferent to, or repelled by others. The meaning of various cultural symbols may be quite different for the various individuals and groups that adopt them. Some people may feel positive toward, or sympathetic with, the cultural complex without taking part in its practices or its social circles. The degree of personal self-conscious commitment to the culture will vary widely.

With these considerations in mind, let us look at some of the major elements of the new youth culture that began to exert a steadily widening appeal to youth of diverse classes, background, and character structure during the sixties.

New Music

The role of music as a medium of cultural and subcultural expression and as a primary means for defining identity is discussed very little in sociological literature. The issue is especially fascinating in the United States because while some ethnic and other subcultures have developed their own indigenous musical forms, a popular music and entertainment industry both disseminates and homogenizes ethnic music continuously.

Since the jazz era of the twenties, white youths have devoted much of their energy, interest, and income to the consumption of pop music. In addition to whatever intrinsic enjoyment may be derived from listening and dancing to it, popular music plays a very important social function as well. The live performance of pop music in dance halls and concerts has, for many years, been the occasion for large, intensely emotional, and uninhibited gatherings of youth. Therefore, it has served as a major stimulus to, and reinforcement of, a sense of common consciousness. Because there are always adults who express revulsion at the explicit sexuality and apparent irrationality that seems to characterize these events, for decades, such occasions have served as mild expressions of defiance of adult authority. Moreover, status in teenage groups often depends on the ability of its members to display their appreciation of currently popular music conspicuously—by attending live performances, collecting records, displaying the right tastes, dancing well, and so on. For a long time, pop music has been an important ingredient in lovemaking, court-ship, and other emotional experiences. As the same music is broad-cast across the country (and to a great extent around the world), it becomes a common frame of reference—a basis for communi-cation and mutual recognition. Moreover, since adults are likely to find the current forms repulsive or unintelligible, pop music is an important means for defining the distinctiveness of one's gen-eration.

I think that one of the most important sources of alienation of intellectual youth from their more conventional peers during the fifties was the quality of the music that was popular among teenagers. It seemed to be entirely a product of tired formulas developed out of Tin Pan Alley. It was always a source of aston-ishment to me that kids in my age group could tolerate—let alone buy—records made by people like Eddie Fisher, Patti Page, and Joni James. In reaction, many young "intellectuals" became "high brows" and cultivated their tastes in classical music. But by the late fifties, a few intellectual, alienated youths invented a kind of popular music that turned out to be a major historical break-through. Out of the intellectual subculture, emerged creative mu-sicians and songwriters who sensed that it was possible to have a music that was both connected to pop and made serious artistic claims, was musically advanced and poetically sophisticated, and expressed the sentiments and experiences of the alienated and in-tellectual subculture.

These young poets and minstrels were heavily influenced by several ethnic musical traditions that were becoming commer-cialized during the fifties—black rhythm and blues, southern blue-grass and rockabilly, urban concert, and coffeehouse folk music. What was ingenious about these young performers was that they found ways to fuse these traditions: they remolded them to fit the needs and tastes of middle class white intellectual young peo-ple, added to this mix efforts at avant-garde poetry and composi-tion, and made an enormously successful popular art form in commercial terms.

The new performers began in essentially two different ways. Some, like Bob Dylan and Joan Baez, got their start by appealing directly to the intellectual subculture on campuses and in city coffeehouses; they began as performers for a special audience and were not regarded as pop stars. Others, especially the British groups, aimed more directly for mass commercial appeal to mainstream teenage audiences.

But I find it fascinating that *both* the folk and the rock performers who became superstars by the mid-sixties tended to have both higher status and more advanced education than any previous generation of pop stars. Most had attended college, or had parents who did, and almost all began their careers by playing for audiences much like themselves; that is, young people with intellectual, educated tastes. This social background was shared by virtually all the white American superstars and musical innovators of the sixties: Bob Dylan, Joan Baez, Jefferson Airplane, the Byrds, the Beach Boys, Janis Joplin, the Doors, James Taylor, and so on. The British groups were more likely to have working class origins, but they had risen out of that background to start art school or college (Mick Jagger attended the London School of Economics).

The contemporary white pop star, then, has markedly different roots from those of his predecessors. Prior to the sixties, pop music, like other aspects of the popular entertainment and sports industries, was an avenue for expression and status for working class and minority youth. It is still possible for lower status youth to gain fame and fortune through pop singing—but only because there remain some distinctive pop music "subcultures"—soul music and country western. Nevertheless, by the mid-sixties, the new music that originated among intellectual youth had become the dominant popular music for white youth of many strata and in many countries.

Not only did the new music dominate the "top forty" lists during the sixties, but the concerts and open-air festivals devoted to its performance attracted crowds of historic proportions by the late sixties. In addition, the record albums and concerts of performers judged too "controversial" or "uncommercial" for standard AM radio play or television appearances were tremendously successful. Moreover, millions of young people in the United States and Europe followed the personal lives of rock "superstars" such as John Lennon, Mick Jagger, Bob Dylan, and Janis Joplin with intense fascination and concern.

Thus, no detailed data or argument is needed to demonstrate

the extensive and intensive popularity of the new music and its performers. For many youths, music became the decisive feature of their lives—the major focus of uncommitted time, money, and energy.

It is also clear that the music, in both its form and its content, was an expression of alienation, group consciousness, and revolt. The form and manner of presentation and the environments of live performance were not only explicitly designed to be an ecstatic *release* from the regulations, routines, and repressions of everyday life, but were intended by the performers to stand as a definite *criticism* and assault upon them. In addition, many performers—often self-consciously—publicly adopted life styles that were unconventional or oppositional. Many represented or advocated mind-expanding drugs, mysticism (and a rejection of Western religion), communal living, sexual freedom, and nonviolence, as well as a variety of more specific social and political causes. Finally, song lyrics, often in very explicit terms, expressed all forms of cultural opposition, social criticism, generational consciousness, and the quest for new cultural identity. Indeed, the fact that serious philosophical, political, and cultural issues were addressed in popular song lyrics and in styles heavily influenced by the literary avant-gardes of the past hundred years was one of the most crucial ways in which the new music was new.

Obviously, however, the difference between the meaning intended by an artist or performer and the meanings given his work by various audiences is substantial. Popularity of the new music does not necessarily signify popularity of the countercultural themes and sentiments that motivated its creators. Indeed, at least one systematic study of the question indicates that many teenagers did not hear the lyrics of popular songs or, if they did, did not attribute general political or cultural meanings to them.

An alternative explanation of the new music's popularity would emphasize both the elaborate machinery of exploitation, publicity, "payola," and other forms of manipulation employed by the entertainment media and the extreme vulnerability of youth to fads and crazes. In its pure form, such an explanation would propose that content of the new musical forms was irrelevant to its success. Rather, the primitive rhythms and simple melodic structure of this music and the personal lives of its performers were appealing because they permitted forms of vicarious unconventionality, release, and revolt that actually reinforce established convention, routines, and norms. Furthermore, the taste of the young is largely manipulated by a combination of public relations, incessant repetition, and the social pressures of an adolescent peer culture.

However, such considerations do not adequately account for the specific content and qualities of the new music and its associated environments and life styles. For example, it is clear in retrospect that the emergence of a highly educated mass audience created a basis for the development of intellectually and aesthetically sophisticated and serious new forms of popular art. In this respect, the new popular music is an aspect of the same process that resulted in the rising popularity of film as a serious art form and the appearance of formerly avant-garde and underground art forms and themes in mass-circulation magazines. In short, one aspect of the cultural change of the past decade has been the emergence of a fused intellectual and popular culture that appeals most directly to the very large educated audience created by mass higher education. Previous barriers between intellectual and popular culture have crumbled substantially not, as some intellectual reformers would have hoped, by inculcation of the masses with high culture or, as intellectual elitists have always feared, by the destruction of serious culture, but by the creation of new art forms and media that synthesize aspects of both high and low culture. Although many teenagers failed to perceive the "newness" of the new music and responded to it as they had to the old, it is obvious that many thousands of youth shared the sensibilities of the young poets and minstrels who composed this music and grasped their meanings and purposes.

We need to know much more than we now do about the bases for the appeal of the new music and the reasons for its profound impact. For example, in addition to the fact that it was more intellectually and artistically serious, new music was intensely expressive of alienation and opposition. To what extent can the widespread acceptance of the new music be attributed to the values that it was designed to express? To which segments of the young were these values and the associated life style immediately appealing? We know almost nothing systematic about such questions as these. All one can say with confidence is that emergence of the new music *popularized* the idea of cultural opposition and generally made available to youth materials for the construction of unconventional identities that had previously been the property of small groups of those we have been calling "intellectual" youth. Whether this fact accounts for the appeal of the new music in any significant degree is still largely a matter of speculation.

Finally, a point to which we shall return. Irrespective of the determinants for the initial diffusion of the new music, it is clear that by the end of the sixties, it plus its associated cultural traits had become almost universally defined—by youth, adults, and the media—as a form of opposition and revolt. If interest in it earlier in the decade had a quite ambiguous significance, this is much less true as this essay is being written.

Hair and the New Fashions

Perhaps even more dramatic than the transformation of musical preferences among youth has been the transformation of fashion. As I have said before, the socially preferred appearance and attire of high school and college males during the mid-fifties were typified by the crew cut and crew neck, slightly scuffed white buck shoes, ivy league cut, and charcoal gray suits. Girls waved their hair and wore shirtwaists, loose sweaters, and skirts or bermuda shorts. In short, the preferred dress accentuated sobriety, cleanliness, and conventionality.

In the emergent intellectual subculture, appearance tended to follow the classic bohemian pattern: males generally appeared neglectful of their attire, wore work clothes, and some grew beards; girls let their hair grow long and wore handcrafted clothing and jewelry and little or no makeup. In general, the emphasis was on the natural and the comfortable.

A more explicit and general revolt against conventional middle class dress was given great impetus by various pop music performers. The Beatles, whose hair was uncommonly long for the time, sparked widespread imitation. By the late sixties, long hair had become characteristic of elite college males and a significant number of high school youths defied school dress regulations in order to sport long sideburns and hair. To complement these changing hair styles, young people adopted a riotous array of unconventional costume-like clothing that bore traces of Indian, cowboy, military, and working class cultures and was overlaid with the brilliant and surrealistic color associated with psychedelic experience. If any generalization about appearance can be made, it was that distinctions in appearance between the sexes were greatly blurred. As boys adopted the long hair, necklaces, headbands, and bright colors that were traditionally feminine, girls bought their clothing in the men's departments and abandoned their makeup.

The underlying meanings of such changing dress fashions are even harder to specify than are the social and psychological roots of the new music.

As hair and dress fashions became more and more widely adopted, it became obvious that many adults were shocked and disturbed by them—again for reasons that are not entirely clear. Many adults and youths felt that the male "costume" was used to express defiance of conventional expectations about the male role. Such costumes represented a direct assault on some of the most basic and problematic assumptions about identity in American culture. In addition, acceptance of such garb as suitable implied a lack of elementary discipline and an aristocratic or feminine attentiveness to personal beauty inappropriate in a culture one is expected to be busy with serious work. In short, the new youth fashions, whatever they might have meant to those who adopted them, quickly became labeled as a direct challenge to deeply held cultural values with respect to the sex role, work, sensuality, and efficient use of time and money. Moreover, since the prevailing fashions were associated in the media with illicit, immoral, and degenerate behavior, it was not surprising that many would quickly assume that individuals who dressed in this fashion were likely to engage in such behavior. Thus, the fully dressed "hippie" youth became a target of verbal insult, physical abuse, and discrimination in many communities. Also, he was likely to experience forms of harassment from law enforcement agencies. In short, to the extent that young people adopted new fashions— even though they may have done so without any significant initial alteration of their commitment to conventional values—they were likely to experience troubles and punishments that resembled those that were experienced by blacks and other racial minorities in urban ghettoes daily.

Drugs

The increasingly common use of marijuana and psychedelic and mood-manipulating drugs on college campuses and among youth in general needs no documentation. Prior to this decade, the illicit use of drugs was commonplace among ghetto youth and minimal among middle-class whites (although fairly prevalent in bohemian circles). Bohemian youth dropout enclaves in the Bay Area and in Manhattan constituted important locales for the spread of psychedelic drugs among white youth. By 1966, rock music groups had emerged from these bohemian drug cultures on both coasts. Not only did they perform, but they also sponsored large outdoor love-ins and indoor light shows that had the total effect of simulating and enchancing the psychedelic experience. These events and explicitly "turned on" music helped popularize the use of marijuana and more potent psychedelic drugs.

As a result of media promotion and underground publicity, by 1967 the Haight-Ashbury district of San Francisco had become—both actually and symbolically—a haven for drug-oriented youth who wanted to live in a manner that was becoming well-known as a total way of life. For a brief period, the Haight symbolized the idea of the "hippie" culture—a way of life in which love, freedom, mysticism, music, youth, and beauty were coupled with mind-expanding and emotionally liberating drugs, communal living, and a "do your own thing" ethic. Thousands of youths flocked to San Francisco to absorb the new culture, then returned to their campuses and towns to spread the myth of Haight-Ashbury. Tens of thousands more shared in their experience from afar and used the myth as a way of legitimizing drug use. Although the Haight myth collapsed, incorporation of marijuana and drugs by the general youth culture was the net result.

The number of young people who regularly use various types of drugs is impossible to estimate and the number who only experiment with drugs is even higher, but the number of those who regard the use of marijuana and related illegal drugs as legitimate probably constitutes a majority. To a very great extent, the widespread use of marijuana was inevitable once it became common-place on campuses and in other locales where youth interact in-tensively. The typically innocuous or euphoric effects of marijuana, its enhancement of social experience, the reduction of anxiety, and the apparent lack of ill effects among friends and acquaintances who use it guaranteed its widespread acceptance. A deeply re-bellious or alienated disposition was no more a factor in the use of grass by large numbers of young people than it had been in the acceptance of new music and hair styles. Grass became a symbol of defiance and revolt almost entirely because its posses-sion and use are illegal. As a result, all users or holders have had some contact with the police or other authorities—either directly or indirectly. For many youths, the illegality of a drug that is either innocuous or, at worst, no more deleterious in its effects than is alcohol, tobacco, or barbiturates is a clear sign of the irrationality and hypocrisy of established authority. There is little evidence that drug use itself is "caused" by more general sentiments of an oppositional or antiauthoritarian character.

Obviously, I have been cautious about arguing that the *spread* of new music, fashion, and drug use was due primarily to the rebellious impulses of those who adopted these new cultural elements. These elements *originated* very largely in the subculture of alienated intellectual students that began to emerge during the late fifties. For this subculture, I would argue, these elements *were* associated with a general antipathy to central aspects of conven-tional culture and functioned to provide new bases for identity formation and collective life for such youth. To a great extent, the rapid diffusion of these cultural elements can be accounted for by the factors discussed in Chapter 3.

First, the new cultural elements emerged at just that point in time when the proportion of youths who were being segregated and herded together in schools, military bases, and urban ghettoes was extremely high. This fact alone helps us understand the reasons that new practices do spread so rapidly. When a sub-stantial number of people who share common problems are thrown together for prolonged periods, ground for the rapid spread of virtually any activity which appears relevant to their common problems is fertile.

Second, the mass media serve a somewhat similar function —a kind of substitute for face-to-face interaction—on a national and international scale. Practices and perspectives which might have diffused very slowly in the past are now broadcast throughout the world and youths who are geographically isolated from centers of the avant-garde are immediately made aware of anything that is new, interesting, pleasurable, or potentially popular.

Most likely, the first youths on any campus or in any community to respond to the new cultural elements were those who confronted most sharply the problems of identity we have attributed to the intellectual and the alienated. The new styles of appearance enabled such young people to make themselves visible to each other and thereby unite to form a local version of the nationally emerging subculture. In many locales, such youth were regarded as deviant, not only by adults, but by those their own age as well. Nevertheless, one important function of the new music and certain kinds of media publicity was to dissolve many of the tensions among peers. Even those who initially did not share the profound cultural alienation of the hippies were likely to share a liking for the Beatles, some respect for their collective visibility, and a desire at least to experiment with marijuana.

Thus, one explanation for the spread of elements of the new youth culture during the sixties ignores the intentional symbolic content of these elements and accounts for their diffusion on the basis of commonplace processes of social influence, group pressure, and contagion. To accept this account in its purest form would lead to the view that virtually any cultural practice widely broadcast and celebrated by the media or repeatedly defined as "popular" or "in" or "the coming thing" by disc jockeys and magazine articles would be widely adopted by young people. The problem with this view is it fails to account for the specific content of that which is celebrated (for example, why have the media felt it necessary to celebrate *alienated* cultural styles and expressions?). If youthful tastes are so easily manipulated, why haven't more conventional "straight" styles, forms, and practices become popularized?

A somewhat more sophisticated account would assume that youth generally are likely to be attracted by particularly hedonistic activities and that they find vicarious experiences of defiance of

convention and authority particularly appealing as forms of emotional release and relief from boredom. Indeed, such impulses are
not restricted to youth, but are experienced most intensely by
white middle class American youth whose daily lives are characterized by regulation, competitive pressure, sexual deprivation,
and dependency. It is not surprising that under these conditions,
counterexperiences, particularly those that are vicarious, are intensely attractive and are part of the normal process of identity
formation and stabilization. From this viewpoint, youth culture,
whether it is conventional or counterconventional, need pose no
threat to established values; indeed, providing youth some opportunity to be released from convention *as youth* may actually
strengthen the hold of established cultural perspectives in the
long run.

It may be that for many youth who attend rock festivals,
wear their sideburns long, and try pot once in a while, the new
youth culture is no more significant than any fad or craze is.
Nevertheless, even fads may have major implications for social
and cultural change. Furthermore, explaining the new culture as
only a fad or craze fails to account for either the emotional intensity of its members, the values they live by and represent, or
the intense conflict this culture has generated in American society.

It is plausible that the cultural elements we have been discussing achieved their popularity for reasons that are deeper and
more historically specific than are those we have emphasized. Perhaps the intellectual and alienated youths of the fifties were more
prophetic than they realized at the time. If their revolt began
primarily in opposition to the prevailing youth culture, it entailed explicit criticism and rejection of the general culture—particularly the Protestant Ethic. If this value syndrome *is* losing its
vitality under the impact of affluence, bureaucratization, and advanced technology (as I argued in Chapter 2), the problems of
identity experienced by intellectual and uncommitted youth are
being experienced in varying degrees by many other young people.
The culture expressed by small and relatively isolated groups of
youth attracted the interest of mainstream youth because all youths
shared problems of self-definition, vocation, and sexual identity.

On the surface, Dylan, long hair, and pot may have satisfied the hedonistic impulses and needs of conventional as well as new youth. They awakened consciousness of the contradictions in a culture in which thrift is a virtue made obsolete by abundance; competitive individualism is inappropriate because the social system maximizes interdependence, coordination, and rational planning; male dominance and aggressiveness and female passivity and dependence cannot coexist with a family and educational system that rests on a considerable degree of sexual equality and in which women are given the central socializing roles.

Relatively few young people may have been able to verbalize contradictions such as these—and our culture embodies many others as well—but by the 1960s the confusions and discontinuities they produced were an integral part of the very character structure and emotional life of millions of American youth.

Moreover, other aspects of the cultural crisis affected large numbers of youth. For instance, many observers have discussed the rapidity of social change as a source of dislocation and "alienation." Since rapid change is inherent in our political economy and social system, they argue, parents and other adults are inescapably inadequate as models of future adult roles for youth. Margaret Mead goes so far as to claim that the peer group is the prime socializing agency in advanced technological society. Furthermore, she argues, we have reached the point where youth constitutes the most viable model of cultural adaptation. In such a "prefigurative" culture, young people are the guides of their elders rather than the reverse.

The result of erosion of traditional values and the rapidity of social change is a situation in which many institutions operate at cross-purposes or are out of phase with each other and considerable conflict within institutions is readily observable. Of all segments of the population, youth, who are attempting to establish a stable identity and personal direction, are most severely affected by cultural incoherence, decay, and transformation.

Although it is hard to demonstrate empirically, it is very plausible, then, to argue that the emergence and spread of an "alienated" youth culture in the sixties was not simply a functional adaptation by "the system" or some ordinary expression of youthful faddishness and exuberance, but rather an expression and a catalyst for profound cultural disintegration and transformation.

If intellectual and "uncommitted" youth were the innovative agents of this cultural change, they were agents because they were least able to accept or be accepted by conventional peer society and, therefore, most vulnerable to cultural strain and most ready for cultural change. If our argument is correct, the problem of identity for youth in our society is not at all marginal or peripheral. It is the direct result of central social and cultural changes that impinge on youth of all strata and character types.

THE EMERGENCE OF STUDENT RADICAL ACTIVISM

The United States has not been as hospitable to left-wing anticapitalist political and social movements as some industrial societies have been. Populist and socialist movements have had a major impact on national and local politics and social reform during some periods, but invariably, the political system and economic growth have had the capacity to absorb and integrate such movements before they could establish permanent roots in the working class or other sectors. As a result, Americans have been relatively apolitical: generally, they supported the political system and typically, they have not linked their personal troubles to the need for major social and political change.

Against this background, it is not at all surprising that the emergent cultural alienation among youth during the fifties should reflect the political indifference that was then general in the society as a whole. Political privatism of the young intellectuals in the fifties was further heightened and reinforced by a mood of conservatism and political pessimism that prevailed among previously politicized adult intellectuals and academics. One source of this mood was the disillusioning effect of Stalinism on the American left, which had become a political factor during the Depression of the thirties. Another source was the conviction that, whatever flaws American culture might possess, the society was relatively humane when placed in the context of fascist and Stalinist barbarism. This mood also stemmed from the wide public attack during the fifties on liberals and intellectuals, as conservative politicians used anticommunist crusades as a means for undermining the mood of social reform that had developed during the

Depression and war years. Finally, postwar prosperity led many intellectuals to feel that the basic ideological issues of industrial society had dissolved, and that the very grounds for political conflict and mobilization in the United States no longer existed.

During the late fifties, every observer of the American campus was likely to comment on the surprising political indifference of American students. Most went on to predict that this apathy was likely to continue, because the society offered a wide array of economic opportunities and because these youths had been reared in a society of general affluence that they expected to attain if not to surpass. It seemed natural that young people, however discontented they might feel with certain aspects of the quality of American life, would not risk their highly promising futures by undertaking political dissent or protest.

In retrospect, a major factor in generating student political disaffiliation probably was the absence of uncorrupted models of effective political action. The Communist Party and its associated political structure, which had mobilized many students during the thirties and forties, had been entirely discredited by such events as the Khrushchev revelations about the Stalin era and the invasion of Hungary. Liberal political organizations and the labor movement, which had also won the support of considerable numbers of students in earlier generations, now seemed bureaucratic and largely quiescent. The faculty and other intellectuals were either highly cautious or cynical about political activism of any sort. Everyday electoral politics appeared either to be devoid of moral content or seriously corrupted. The critical mood that prevailed in the emerging campus intellectual subculture could not be stably contained in a posture of social withdrawal, especially since many intellectual youth, as we have pointed out, had been raised to have a sense of social responsibility. Nevertheless, there were no means of political expression that were both effective and morally valid.

Then, on February 2, 1960, four Negro students in Greensboro, North Carolina "sat-in" at a segregated lunch counter. Almost immediately, the sit-in movement spread throughout the South, as hundreds of black students found a way of directly undermining segregation in public facilities. Within a short time, a black student movement took form in the South. In uneasy alliance with the minister-based nonviolent movement led by Martin

Luther King, the black students created a broad, many-pronged movement against legal segregation and for full citizenship for southern Negroes.

Almost immediately, a response to southern sit-ins was heard on a number of northern campuses. White students picketed local branches of five-and-ten-cent stores that practiced segregation in the South. Support groups for the Student Non-violent Coordinating Committee sprouted on many campuses, and white students began to trek South to participate in freedom rides, voter registration campaigns, and other supportive activities.

It is not entirely clear why sit-ins "triggered" white young radicalism. Evidence suggests that those who responded to this movement were members of the campus intellectual subculture. Why did the sit-ins have such an impact on young white "intellectuals"?

First, the sit-ins were a very dramatic demonstration of the major failure of America's democratic claims—failure to guarantee the constitutional rights and elementary conditions of citizenship of southern Negroes. This failure and the profound injustices that were its results, were a crystallization not only of the more abstract discontents that intellectual youths felt about the moral hypocrisies of the society but about its political stagnation as well. Also they highlighted the *privileged*-position of white students dramatically: since many student intellectuals had been reared with considerable guilt about their status and disdained material success, such a demonstration was particularly compelling for them.

Second, the sit-ins occurred in the context of international events in which students played an effective role in shaping history. Recently, students had overthrown military dictatorships in Turkey and South Korea through militant street demonstrations; they had blocked the visit of President Eisenhower to Japan, and they had played a central role in the victorious Cuban revolution.

The sit-ins and the black student movement seemed to be part of a general historical process in which students, *acting in their role as students,* had become effective agents of social change. Instead of waiting for leadership from other elements in the society to promote social reform, students themselves could actually have historical effects.

Third, the sit-ins and the southern movement as a whole involved the use of profoundly moral means to attain profoundly moral ends. Indeed, rarely has there been a social movement in which means and ends were so intimately connected. The civil rights movement seemed free of the brutality, manipulation, and callousness that political action had been assumed to require during the fifties.

Forms of pacifist direct action that SNCC, King, and other civil rights leaders advocated and practiced were seen by white intellectual students as ways of living one's values and simultaneously changing the world. They seemed to be genuine breakthroughs beyond the classic dilemma of *moral purity v. practical action*. Moreover, one could be for civil rights without being concerned with the generalized political ideology and thereby avoid all the sour dilemmas of cold war politics.

Fourth, the five-and-dime picketing brought student intellectuals together around a political issue and generated social interaction over political and social problems. Once such groups became aware of their capacity for collective action, it was quite unlikely that they would dissipate. The concept of the student as an agent of social change, modeled on the actions of Latin American and Asian student movements, took root very quickly.

It is useful to consider the American student movement as having passed through roughly three major phases. Each phase was quite distinct from the previous one in many respects; each new phase was the result largely of the interaction between the movement and the political authority structure. In each phase, the movement grew in size and scope, became more radical ideologically, and more militant tactically.

I now review these phases schematically. This is not the place for a detailed or fully rounded history of the American student movement. Rather my analysis is designed to see how its development was associated with historical events and processes to which students reacted.

Phase I: Pacifism, Protest, and Reform, 1960–64

As I have suggested, during the first years of the sixties, increasing numbers of white students became involved in the civil rights movement. The most dramatic forms of commitment were displayed by the hundreds who "went South" to join the struggle directly as actionists and organizers. Hundreds of other students worked in northern ghettoes in tutorial programs and direct action campaigns against job and housing discrimination. Throughout these years, the appeal of the civil rights cause was based not only on the just aims of the movement, but on the perception of the black actionists as saintly heroes who received harsh brutality but returned love, and who were viewed as the conscience of the nation.

In these years, nonviolent direct action and passive resistance were seen as radical weapons in a struggle for social reform. On the one hand, they appeared as tactically appropriate means for a physically weak minority to force society to fulfill its professed ideals. On the other hand, pacifist action projected a vision of society in which the threat and use of force could be replaced by exchange and cooperation as the basis for social relations. Finally, passive resistance and civil disobedience were appealing because they could be employed effectively by small groups and by individuals and because they enabled the activist to act effectively without having to wait for collective decisions to sanction his actions.

Direct-action tactics applied by small groups of pacifists to issues other than civil rights paralleled the nonviolent civil rights movement. In particular, a movement opposed to the arms race, nuclear testing, civil defense and other manifestations of the cold war was gaining widespread support. This loosely organized movement in which students from "intellectual" campuses such as Harvard, Swarthmore, Michigan, and Brandeis played an active role relied largely on mass marches, vigils, and other forms of legal protest. Some civil disobedience occurred—for example radical pacifists attempted to board Polaris submarines and to sail small boats into nuclear testing areas while New York college students defied civil authority by refusing to take part in civil defense shelter drills. In 1962, hundreds of students became involved in congressional campaigns of "peace" candidates—the most dramatic being the third party senatorial campaign of Harvard Professor H. Stuart Hughes in Massachusetts.

During these years, small groups of campus intellectuals intensively debated the viability of student political activism as a basis for a general "new politics" in the United States. Within a year after the southern sit-ins had begun, numerous little magazines and campus political discussion groups had sprouted at major universities and colleges. Several interrelated themes were topics of all these discussions: the need for intellectuals to become politically engaged, the inadequacy of classical political ideologies and categories for guiding political action, and the need for new theory or ideology to provide a general social analysis and critique and the basis for a new political program.

By 1962, interest in developing a general political thrust among students had led to formation of the Students for a Democratic Society that announced its hope for what it called a "new left" (a term that its founders had borrowed from a comparable British group of radicals who had broken with both communist and traditional labour politics) and issued a manifesto containing many of the elements for constructing a new radicalism.

In its beginnings, the new left neither envisioned a mass student movement nor imagined that students, by themselves, would be primary agents of social change. Instead it hoped for an alliance for social reform that would combine elements of the labor movement, liberal political reformers, the civil rights movement, liberal churches and students and intellectuals—a movement that would use both direct action and the electoral process to build a political base for achieving racial equality, eliminating domestic poverty, ending the arms race and the cold war, and building a more democratically organized social order. These early student activists defined their on-campus role as educating their fellow students to the need for political engagement and support of civil rights and other off-campus reform movements. For them, the most virtuous role for the student activist was seen as getting off the campus and becoming involved directly in "real" social problems.

The early new left's optimism about the possibilities for societal reform was reinforced by its perception of the Kennedy administration. Admiration of John Kennedy as president was a factor less important than was the belief that his administration would be necessarily responsive to the pressure for reform being applied by Negroes, labor, and the universities (obviously, the administration's political base depended heavily on these constituencies). Essentially, the early young radicals believed in the necessity and efficacy of grassroots pressure in impelling established institutions and the government to move in progressive directions. Research on the social origins of the early student activists strongly supports our view that, overwhelmingly, they were sons and daughters of "intellectual" and liberal parents who saw the activity of their offspring as fulfilling, rather than rebelling against, their families' tradition of social concern. Typically, they shared with their parents a reverence of the university; like their parents, they found organized religion an inadequate source of values, and perhaps even more than their parents, they identified the university as the sole established institution in the society that could facilitate the search for new values and meanings and help define a morally coherent and humanistic way of life. Far from wishing to destroy the university, radical students were among the most committed to its fulfillment as a central institution in their lives. Many expected eventually to end up as university faculty or as intellectuals associated with the academic community; they hoped it would become a place hospitable to the grassroots movements for change with which they also identified.

Activist students sustained many sharp disillusionments during the Kennedy years. The Cuban invasion, the missile crisis, and other incidents of great international tension. These events seemed to confirm the view—enunciated several years before by the maverick sociologist C. Wright Mills—that enormous power, including the power to destroy humanity, was vested in the hands of a tiny group of men who were substantially irresponsible, and that this situation was intolerable. A further source of disillusionment was the federal government's posture in relation to the civil rights movement in the South. The Justice Department often was extremely cautious or negligent about protecting the persons and rights of civil rights workers and about enforcing elementary constitutional rights in the deep South. Moreover, the Kennedy forces refused to mount a frontal attack to challenge the power of southern segregationists within the Democratic Party and in Congress.

Such disillusionments were balanced by certain positive trends. By the summer of 1963, the United States and the Soviet Union were moving toward a détente symbolized by the nuclear test ban agreement, and the undertone of President Kennedy's speeches represented a marked departure from traditional cold war rhetoric. At the same time, a reform coalition for civil rights and domestic equality—symbolized by the massive march on Washington, in August 1963—seemed to be emerging. At the time of Kennedy's assassination in November, 1963, his death did not appear to affect this general situation. In Lyndon Johnson's first year as president, many of the legislative demands of the civil rights movement were enacted, and a general war on poverty was announced. A period of domestic reform seemed definitely in process. Furthermore, a relaxation of the threat of nuclear war was evident.

During 1963 and 1964, thousands of students became actively involved in the reform effort. Thousands attempted to relate to northern urban ghettoes, to Appalachia, and to the campaign in the South to build black political strength. Thousands volunteered for the Peace Corps. At the time, many of these voluenteers hopefully defined the Corps as a possible replacement of military conscription and intervention overseas. Such volunteer commitments were sponsored by institutions such as government agencies and private foundations. Involvements that were more politically focused and activist were mobilized by SNCC, SDS, and other radical and civil rights groups.

In 1964, these efforts culminated in the Mississippi Summer Project, which attracted at least 1,000 northern white students for fulltime voter registration and related activity in some of the most oppressed counties in the United States. At the beginning of the summer, three volunteers were murdered by a racist gang; still, student volunteers worked throughout the summer, and many stayed on for a longer period.

Creation of an integrated alternative to the segregated Mississippi Democratic party was one aspect of strategy involved in the Mississippi campaign. It was hoped that the Freedom Democrats could win recognition as the official Mississippi delegation to the Democratic convention. Mainly, the campaign ended in bitter disillusionment. Students were shocked by their first-hand experience with southern justice and rural poverty. Black activists were disturbed by the white students' tendency to dominate and patronize. Ultimately, many participants concluded that the cause of black self-determination was one that blacks must control and from which whites must be excluded as coequal participants.

Both black and white civil rights activists were deeply embittered by failure of the Democratic Convention in Atlantic City in August, 1964 to recognize the effort for which they had risked so much; they were particularly embittered by liberal Democrats who had taken the lead in urging them to compromise their political goals in the interest of Democratic Party unity.

For many members of the growing student and black movements, this Democratic Convention represented a profound turning point. Four years of effort to galvanize established liberal and moderate political efforts for fundamental reform within the framework of the formal political system and to form a national coalition of labor, blacks and liberals had not produced the desired effects. Goals of southern civil rights had been legislated on paper, but the realization of these goals, in terms of full citizenship for the black population, seemed as far off as it ever had been.

By summer 1964, black protest had moved to the urban North and violent insurrection had overshadowed nonviolent direct action. Early new leftists had realized that the only alternative to taking to the streets was a broadly based political movement that would directly challenge the entrenched power of racist, commercial, militarist, and reactionary interests that effectively blocked the socioeconomic changes necessary for racial equality. Labor and liberal leadership had the capacity to mobilize such a movement, but by 1964 this possibility seemed far less likely than it had when the decade opened.

Parenthetically, it is interesting to note that the "new politics" advocated by the new left in the early sixties was not seriously undertaken until the 1968 presidential primaries, when a few liberal politicians embodied this concept. Significantly, thousands of youths enthusiastically participated in the McCarthy and Kennedy campaigns.

Had the new politics been mobilized four years earlier, patterns of youth behavior might well have taken a fundamentally different path. Instead, as the summer of '64 ended, the most actively engaged student activists felt a deepening sense of frustration with and isolation from established institutions.

Moreover, as the southern struggle for desegregation and civil rights culminated, the black movement entered a new phase. Its youthful wing oriented increasingly toward black urban ghetto youth and away from integration, nonviolence and simple visions of brotherhood and the beloved community. Black militants had become disillusioned not only with the political system, but with white students as necessary collaborators. Their message to the white new left: don't keep organizing us, make your own struggle for social change among your own people. Thus, by the end of 1964 many of the initial assumptions and modes of action of the emerging white student movement had been substantially undermined by the pressure of external events.

Phase II: Confrontation, Radicalization, and Resistance, 1964–68

The 1964–65 academic year began under dramatic circumstances. At the Berkeley campus of the University of California, thousands of students engaged in rallies, sit-ins and other demonstrations to protest administration maneuvering to prevent the use of a strip of university-owned sidewalk by the political groups for the purpose of recruiting participants for off-campus political action.

The Free Speech Movement was the first large-scale mass movement of students to use direct action to change the policies of university administrators. It represented a successful effort to utilize the tactics and spirit of the civil rights movement in relation to university issues. The FSM culminated in a mass seizure of the administration building at Berkeley by a mass of students, establishment of a "free university" in the building that lasted for many hours, clearance of the building by the state highway patrol at the governor's order, and arrest of approximately 800 students. These events were followed by a university-wide strike and a vote by the Faculty Senate to meet the basic demands of the FSM.

Berkeley had a profoundly transforming effect on the student movement for several reasons. First, it demonstrated that although committed activists might comprise only a small fraction of the student body on a day-to-day basis, most students can be persuaded to join actions that they define as being in their interest. Furthermore, it was clear that at Berkeley the subculture that provided the immediate constituency of the movement had grown substantially in a relatively short time. Second, the public impact of Berkeley suggested that the campus was not irrelevant to major social conflict, as most new leftists had assumed, but might well be a major arena of struggle. Berkeley dramatized the fact that the university had itself been transformed during the fifties and was now intimately and fundamentally connected to the major centers of power and political initiative in the larger society: It was an important element in the defense establishment; its educational function was decisive in providing the manpower to operate the corporate and governmental organizational structure; its policies regarding admissions, personnel, curriculum, and research had substantial effects on change related to blacks and other ethnic minorities; and its internal life and administrative structure symbolized the general social consequences of bureaucratization just as the gap between its rhetorically proclaimed ideals and its actual practice typified the chasm between the ideal and the real that prevailed in the society as a whole. Such a representation was particularly painful to intellectual, socially concerned students, who, as we have seen, had hoped that the university would symbolize an *alternative* to the prevailing culture and social order, rather than merely reflect and submit to dominant values, trends and interests.

The Berkeley FSM and the enormous amount of discussion and analysis that it generated dramatized for the new left the possibility that one did not have to go South or into the ghetto to confront the basic problems of society. Indeed, as black activists had argued, it might be more authentic to fight one's own battles on one's own turf. Not incidentally, such a changed perspective was reinforced by the startling observation that such a tactic could be more effective in gaining student participation than off-campus actions had been. For less politicized students, Berkeley served to raise fundamental questions about the nature of university education. As we have seen, in addition to the committed activists, a rather broad group of students confronted basic problems of value and identity. Perhaps to many of them it had been obvious that university education was quite inadequate in helping them cope with such issues, but that something might be done to change the situation had not been.

After Berkeley, "university reform" activities swept through American campuses. Some of these were sparked by the organized new left, but most were not. In the period immediately following the confrontation at Berkeley, such activity did not take the form primarily of overt protest; instead, "free universities" and other experimental educational activity became widespread, student political parties were formed and petitions circulated, and rallies and picket lines became commonplace as students pressed for a greater voice in university governance and sought an end to restrictive regulations on social life and political activity.

Meanwhile, in early 1965, the Johnson administration initiated the systematic bombing of North Vietnam and sent American combat troops into South Vietnam in force. The Tonkin Gulf bombings and congressional resolutions of August 1964 had confirmed intimations that the war would be escalated, and on many major campuses, concern and debate about Vietnam increased—a concern that had been sparked considerably by several leading academic figures. Almost immediately after escalation became a fact, faculty and student groups on a large number of campuses initiated teach-ins that were prolonged, intense discussions and debates about Vietnam and were aimed at stimulating a national process of debate over administration war policy. SDS called for a national student march on Washington in April, 1965, and much to the surprise of the organizers, some 25,000 students participated—by far, the largest national student protest activity in the United States since the 1930s. In a short time, a "university perspective" of the war had developed. This perspective—based partially on the intensive analyses of Vietnam and foreign policy specialists and partially on careful reading of major newspaper reports on Vietnam—incorporated the following convictions: the war was fundamentally a civil war in which the United States had neither the moral right nor the practical capacity to successfully intervene; United States intervention was illegal under international agreements and the United States Constitution; United States military activity and bombing involved an immoral devastation of civilians; the United States was siding with a brutal military regime that had no popular base against an insurgent nationalist movement that did and that such a stance was both impractical and immoral; and United States interests were not involved in Vietnam and even if they were, the most hardheaded analysis would show that any gains for United States interests would be offset by the damage to our international position that prolonged involvement would entail. Not only did the administration and its spokesmen rarely deal with the substance of these analyses, but often, administration claims and arguments were falsified by journalistic reports and subsequent events.

Instead of responding to rising protest in a positive fashion, the administration steadily escalated its involvement in the war. Increasingly, both students and distinguished professors questioned the rationality, veracity, and democratic responsiveness of the administration. Mass public rallies steadily increased in size, and on campus, bitterness with the administration grew. Increasingly, the new left argued that the war was not an "error" of policy, but a built-in consequence of the imperialist-militarist organization of American society. Increasingly, such arguments were received attentively by less politicized university people. Meanwhile, the American domestic crisis was dramatized and intensified by an accelerating number of ghetto riots and by an increasingly militant rhetoric and organizational thrust in the black community. The war and the military priority were identified more and more on campus as major barriers to urgently needed domestic social reform

For increasing numbers of students, especially the activists, these events were having a radicalizing effect. In this context, radicalization meant, above all, a shift in the definition of the political situation away from the view that popular protest and pressure could lead toward positive change and toward the view that the dominant elites were not open to democratic pressure, that they exercized authority illegitimately, and that trust could not be placed in conventional political processes. In this situation, changes in tactics were felt to be urgent. Domestic costs of waging war had to be raised   particularly the costs of mobilizing young men to fight the war. Furthermore, the illegitimate character of the war justified and necessitated forms of civil disobedience that would force the authorities to choose between violent repression of dissent or accommodation to it. Such confrontation could also expose to uncommitted people the underlying brutality of the society's managers.

A major precipitant of such radicalization occurred in the Spring of 1966, when Selective Service Director Lewis Hershey announced that student deferments from the draft would henceforth be based on the academic standing of students. This decision (which, ironically, was never implemented) occurred in the context of startling revelations about the involvement of universities in government-sponsored covert intelligence operations in Vietnam and elsewhere and in research on germ warfare and other weapons as well as in dramatic exposés about the penetration of the CIA into domestic student and academic organizations and activities.

For student radicals, university complicity with militarism offered the opportunity to combine student power and antiwar energies and of implementing a strategy of resistance to the war within the institutions of society. On campus, occupation of administration buildings on many campuses served to urge universities to refuse to comply with draft board demands for student class rankings. Almost overnight, the draft became a major issue on campus. Students quickly became conscious of the use of Selective Service as an instrument for channeling youth educationally and vocationally. They perceived conscription as a primary source of competitive pressure among youth and as a mechanism for caste-like stratification of the youth population. The idea of resistance to the draft spread rapidly; by Spring, 1967, hundreds of draft cards had been burned or turned back to draft boards and the number of young men who publicly refused to serve was rising. Public opinion polls indicated that the majority of graduating seniors were contemplating either evading the draft or refusing to recognize its legitimacy; thousands of youths sought to emigrate to Canada rather than face the draft.

Meanwhile, campus confrontations concerning university relations to military institutions became commonplace. Students worked to block military and defense industry recruitment on campus and disrupted university functions in protest over war-related research.

In October, 1967, nearly 100,000 youthful demonstrators converged on the Pentagon. The rising spirit of resistance to the war was symbolized by these demonstrators who sat down illegally on the Pentagon steps and were met with a night of mass arrests and occasionally brutal beatings. Simultaneously, in Oakland, California thousands of students spent a week disrupting the functioning of the Induction Center. Their actions were highlighted by overt resistance to the police, mobile street tactics, and barricades. The temper of the campuses had become so bitter that few administration officials could peacefully address college audiences; the president could not appear in public without almost certain exposure to hostile demonstrations.

Since the advent of Vietnam protests, the organized student left had grown enormously. The SDS, which had barely 20 functioning chapters in 1963, was represented on at least 350 campuses by 1968 and claimed a participating membership in the tens of thousands.

A *Fortune Magazine* survey conducted in late 1968 suggested that about 10 percent of the total American student body identified with the new left. On each major campus, hundreds of students were ready to be mobilized for mass actions and thousands more typically empathized with their positions, although they avoided or opposed disruptive demonstrations and direct confrontations.

Underlying the intensifying radicalization and militance were continuing escalation of the war and the growing conviction that disruption was the only method of effecting a change in policy or, at least, of galvanizing moderate political forces into opposition to the war. Radicalization was reinforced by instances of arbitrary and brutal police activity against demonstrations. Moreover, as increasing numbers of youth adopted the styles and orientations of the youth culture and used drugs, they were met with police harassment and public abuse. By 1966, the protest-folk music and hard rock styles had fused, and the sounds and lyrics that were most widely popular contained increasingly heavy undertones of alienation and hostility. Many apolitical youths were attracted by the new music and by drugs. As their identification with the youth culture increased, so did their identification with one or another form of cultural alienation or political opposition.

Leading spokesmen and gurus of the youth culture continued to derogate political protest and emphasize the superiority of "dropping out" and "doing your own thing"; many apolitical youth undoubtedly agreed. Thus, a certain tension within the youth culture persisted between "politicoes" and "hippies," although the radicalization of the latter and the hair of the former were evidently growing.

By the spring of 1968, the situation seemed likely to change. The antiwar candidacy of Eugene McCarthy and the emergence of Bobby Kennedy in direct opposition to Johnson led to the latter's withdrawal from the presidential race and an outpour of student involvement in the primary races. McCarthy's "children crusade" was composed of many adherents of the new left, but primarily it was not an alternative to the streets—as the candidate liked to fancy. Rather, it represented involvement in politics of tens of thousands of students who had not been activists before.

But hopes for a "new politics" within the American mainstream were soon dashed by the assassination of its two most charismatic proponents—Martin Luther King, Jr. and Robert Kennedy—and the evident strength of Richard Nixon and Hubert Humphrey within the regular party machinery. The primary results provided evidence that public opinion favored an end to the Vietnam war, but the political system seemed organized to prevent the reflection of such popular opinion in presidential nominees and party platforms.

Meanwhile, a revolt of black students and SDS at Columbia University resulted in the prolonged seizure of several university buildings and a rhetorical militance unprecedented on American campuses. The Columbia militants proclaimed revolutionary objectives (rather than university reform or student power) as their real intentions. They were met by a particularly brutal police response, the ferocity of which stunned the attentive academic community across the country. The Columbia events were followed shortly in time by the French general strike that was catalyzed by Columbia-like building seizures at the Sorbonne and other universities and fierce street-fighting in the Latin Quarter. The fact that a student uprising could set off a general strike and threaten the De Gaulle regime reinforced the already developing revolutionary consciousness of many new left activists in the United States.

Once again a Democratic Party presidential convention marked a major turning point for the new radicalism of the sixties. The slim possibility that the convention might recognize the antiwar movement in its platform and candidacies provided hope for more moderate youth. Others thought that the candidates might be swayed by massive street demonstrations. More radical activists agreed on the desirability of mass demonstrations, but mainly as a way of dramatizing the undemocratic character of the political system. By the time of the Convention, fears of a "bloodbath" kept thousands away from Chicago; the relatively small number who came were met by an extremely brutal and repressive police response that was fully and internationally telecast.

As 1968 drew to a close, it was clear that discontent and radicalization permeated both the campus and the black ghettoes. The opportunities the year had presented to channel this discontent back into the political system had been lost. As youthful rebelliousness increased, so did hostility toward it. Radicalism among white youth was still predominantly the expression of those with intellectual origins and aspirations, but the events of the previous eight years had demonstrated that this segment of youth was far more extensive than anyone had previously thought and far more capable of having an impact on wider circles of young people than new left ideologues had, for the most part, imagined. That impact was, in large measure, a consequence of the general cultural crisis of American society, but its profound *radicalization* was attributable to the incapacity of established liberal and moderate forces to promote effective social reform. The failure of reform had several interrelated consequences.

First, and most important, it was central to the delegitimation of the political system and of established authority generally. To accept a political system—especially when its outcomes run counter to the interests of one's group—requires that it convincingly demonstrate its openness and potential responsiveness to personal grievances, demands and aspirations. This is especially pressing at a time of crisis, when many individuals feel that their very lives are endangered by a continuation of existing policies. That reform-minded politicians and administrators repeatedly called upon youth to "work within the system" was not helpful to maintaining its overall legitimacy when efforts to do so were met with total rejection in a context of urgency and many moderate leaders seemed unready to take the necessary political risks to improve the chances for positive change. All of this was symbolized very clearly by the Democratic convention of 1968.

A second consequence of the failure of reform is that it sharpened generational conflict. A historically validated generalization is that generational revolt is most likely to occur when *adult* political reform movement and activity is weak. Generational conflict expressed through collective action is neither inevitable nor the result of repressed Oedipal impulses. The history of the new left in the United States, and student movements elsewhere, suggests that *hostility toward the older generation becomes fully manifest when substantial segments of the adult generation do not use available opportunities to oppose the existing regime and to promote social reform. When adult reform movements are vigorously active, youth are more likely to join them than to seek independent means of political expression.*

Phase III: Beyond Student Protest

Trends in youth consciousness evident in 1968—increasing politicization and radicalization—continued and the student movement underwent further transformations during 1969 and 1970.

First, the organization and militance of black youth crystallized in two ways. On many campuses, the increasing number of black youths at major universities resulted in the formation of militant and disciplined Black Student Unions, which used the threat of disruption and the guilt of white faculty and administrators to win concessions with respect to cultural recognition for blacks within university curricula, a measure of black student control over relevant university resources, and positive changes in university admissions and hiring policies to increase black participation. Meanwhile, in the urban ghettoes, the Black Panther Party spread its influence among school and street youth in the direction of "armed self-defense" against police occupation and explicitly revolutionary organization within the black community.

The new left, from its inception, had followed the leadership of the black youth movements; in this instance, the impact of the BSU and the Panther Party was to reinforce and intensify the developing revolutionary mood among organized student radicals.

But it was far easier to express a revolutionary mood through rhetoric, posters, and other symbolic means than it was to work out its concrete political meaning. In this period, SDS broke into extremely hostile factions as it tried to cope with the following ironic situation: its constituency among youth appeared very large and growing, but many SDS ideologues mistrusted the "revolutionary commitment" of youth; on the other hand, it was clear that revolutionary spirit was restricted to youth and no basic social transformation could occur without the support or acceptance of the majority of Americans. Out of this dilemma arose factions that differed sharply over the relevance of the youth revolt to "revolution," over the relevance of the industrial working class, and over other fundamental issues of strategy and tactics. The outcome of this internal conflict in the new left was the demise of SDS as a national organization. By summer of 1970, no national organization had the capacity to speak for white radicals or to mobilize radical activism.

Meanwhile, mass confrontations on the campus were becoming increasingly costly for participants as a result of severe police attacks, court sentences, and suspensions and expulsions from the schools.

During the 1969–70 school year, despite the dissolution of the organized new left and despite the increased costs of protests, the scope and intensity of student and youth protest reached its peak. Student protest tended to shift from the campus to the surrounding youth "ghettoes," and street fighting, "trashing," and burning became visibly more prevalent than nonviolent civil disobedience was. An underground composed of small guerilla-like bands emerged, claiming responsibility for a growing wave of bombings of military installations, corporate headquarters, banks, and ROTC buildings. Police and national guard occupations and terrorization of campuses and youth ghettoes became increasingly common.

Dissatisfaction during the 1970 school year culminated in the Cambodian invasion, an event that sparked an unprecedented nationwide strike of students. The strike was spurred by the killing of students in Ohio and Mississippi by national guardsmen and police. The national strike revealed the extent of student opposition to the war and disaffection with the political system as hundreds of schools were closed for several days and hundreds of thousands of previously inactive students took part in an enormous variety of strike-related activity, joined by thousands of faculty members and in some cases even by the staffs of school administrations. Most of this activity was essentially nonviolent and nonconfrontational— it involved an enormous amount of lobbying, canvassing and other efforts to reach out beyond the campus to the presumably anti-student public. But confrontation and violence did occur on a substantial proportion of campuses during the weeks of striking— including campuses that had previously experienced little or no overt unrest.

By the end of the school year, several things were evident. The campus shift to the left on the war—and on other issues as well—was massive. At the same time, there seemed to be a rising tide of public hostility to students, hippies, and protesters—a hostility assiduously exploited by the Administration and by local politicians. Finally, it appeared that students, acting as students, could have an effect on national policy: for instance, it was widely believed that the Cambodian invasion was limited by the intensity of the youthful reaction to it —but this effect was modest considering the emotion, energy, and organization that had given rise to the national strike.

By the summer of 1970, many believed that the universities and the government were on a collision course and that growing civil strife was in the offing. Many expected that the new school year would bring an escalation of the campus crisis, the closing of universities, more youth rioting, and deaths. As the congressional election campaign heated up, certain politicians used the "students" and "law and order" as prime issues, and columnists widely predicted conservative electoral triumphs because of adult backlash. Prior to the elections, it seemed that the public was about to give a mandate to escalated repression of dissent, of universities, and of youth.

In fact, however, such a mandate was not forthcoming from the electorate. Many "law and order" candidates were defeated; Congress remained firmly in Democratic control; and Democrats swept gubernatorial contests in many states. In California, Governor Ronald Reagan, who had based much of his political thrust for several years on a hardline policy toward students and the university, was returned to office with a significantly reduced margin of victory and despite weak opposition. At the same time, the Democrats took control of the California legislature. In short, the 1970 elections suggested that a politics of repression did not have sufficient appeal to the electorate to offset public concern with more personally urgent economic issues or to fundamentally disrupt conventional voting patterns.

Meanwhile, a new mood seemed to be emerging on the campus and among youth generally. As the Fall semester of 1970 opened, the sense of imminent revolution seemed to be receding. Among young radicals, there was increasing criticism of bombing and other guerilla activity and an increasing tendency to seek forms of political action that would bridge the isolation of the Movement from other sectors of the population. As opinion polls showed growing public opposition to the war and growing popular anxiety over the economy, many Movement adherents argued that violent tactics were self-defeating. They contended that radicalized youth had more in common with discontented adults than had previously been thought, but that these potential allies were alienated by campus confrontation and terrorism. Even the Weathermen —the underground SDS faction that had been claiming credit for many major bombings—confessed to having overemphasized the military dimension of the struggle and called for a new strategy that would emphasize organizing and educating uncommitted people.

These changes in the perspectives of organized radicals were comparable to changes in the more general campus mood. Many concerned students had come to feel that both "peaceful protest" and "revolution now" strategies were either futile or counterproductive. As a result, there was a noticeable withdrawal of many from active political participation, a decline in dramatic protest activity, and a shift away from action to introspection, self-expression and privatism.

Many interpreted the decline of student militance as a result of repression—that is, the strict enforcement of legal penalties against civil disobedience, an increase in the use of force against demonstrators, and an increase in the covert surveillance of the campus by police agencies. But it would be too simple to assert that students were fearfully retreating in the face of overwhelming force.

The force was undoubtedly there, and there is no question that radical activists felt increasingly threatened, restricted, and spied upon and that many left-oriented students increasingly wondered whether expressions of overt dissidence were worth the possible personal consequences, but countertendencies were also evident. For example, as I have suggested, hard-line politicians were not winning the expected popular support. There was little evidence of a building public consensus in favor of a harsh crackdown; in fact, the concern of the "silent majority" was far more evidently directed against the war and unemployment than it was against the protesters.

Furthermore, government efforts at repression were less than uniformly effective. Public exposure of undercover surveillance activity by the army and the FBI led to widespread opposition to such government practices. In several crucial trials of Black Panthers and other militants, juries refused to return convictions. A rising tide of vocal criticism of the Justice Department, the FBI, and the police was emanating from Congress, the media, and other centers of established opinion. In the summer of 1970, after Cambodia, Kent State, Jackson State, and so forth, virtually all observers assumed that the youth and the state were on a frightening collision course and that the adult majority was lining up behind the state. A year later, it appeared that the collision had temporarily been averted. Presumably, the threat of social disaster had resulted in reconsideration on all sides.

Young activists began an intense process of reassessment of strategy and tactics. The wider mass of disaffected youth remained deeply mistrustful of established authority and the political system, but many continued to hope for an answer from within the system.

As I write this, it appears that several new developments are likely to be decisive in shaping the future of radicalism and youth politics in America. Among these are: the rise of youth "ghettoes"; the emergence of organized resistance in the military; the sharp constriction of employment opportunities for college-educated youth; the 18 year old vote; a renewed interest among radicals in both electoral politics and nonviolent direct action; the Women's Liberation Movement; and signs of renewed militance among workers. I will consider some probable consequences of these developments in Chapter 5.

Before we try to look into the future however, it seems necessary that some of the implications of the history of student protest I have just tried to sketch be considered. So, by way of summary and interpretation here are some general propositions about the rise of student radicalism in the sixties that seem to be derivable from the historical sketch I have drawn:

1. Political radicalism among American youth was rooted in the rise of a new social stratum—the mass intellegentsia whose social position, shared values, and personal aspirations made them unusually ready for political activism and social reformism. Thus, an overwhelming number of the first white youths to become acti-

vated in the sixties had been born into this stratum and raised to
be socially concerned.

2. Students born into older social strata were activated early
in the sixties to the extent that (a) they aspired to become members
of the intelligentsia; (b) they shared problems of identity similar
to those of "intellectual" youth. Many more students had these
characteristics than most researchers had realized.

3. Grouping of large masses of youth in large universities
was a critical structural condition for mass politicization and radicalism. This situation freed youth to devote time and energy to
social issues. It created an excellent opportunity for intense interaction over such issues and for the development of a broad
collective consciousness concerning such issues. Furthermore,
the universities served as political microcosms within which political conflict could be conducted on a scale small enough so that individuals and small groups could feel that they were having effects.
Furthermore, the increasing centrality of the universities to the
functioning of the society as a whole meant that such local conflicts had a wide social and historical impact.

4. Thus, in retrospect, rise of a student movement and emergence of internal conflict within the university seem to have been
an inevitable consequence of the creation of a system of a mass
higher education. The student movement, in its early phase, did
not enunciate revolutionary aims, and it was decidedly an expression of a minority of the student body. It is therefore plausible that
both the student movement and the "intellectual" youth culture
could have been incorporated as "functional" components of the
ongoing system and served as sources of creative tension to facilitate
the progressive modernization of education, politics and mass culture, while restricted in membership to a minority and managed to prevent extreme polarization. Instead, however, an initially
reformist movement became avowedly revolutionary; an initially
"deviant" subculture became the dominant one on the campus.

5. These transformations of the student movement are a
consequence of what may be the single most important development of the sixties in the United States—the decline in the legitimacy of the established political system. An authority structure is
legitimate to the extent that those living under it perceive those
in authority as deserving of their positions, as rightfully fulfilling

their duties, as giving orders that are proper and obligatory, and as capable of being influenced by the use of established procedures. In the United States, the fundamental ground of such legitimacy is the perception that those who govern authentically express the will of the majority, that they protect the rights of minorities, and that their policies will be designed to provide for the progressive improvement of the well-being of the people as a whole.

SOME REASONS FOR DECLINING LEGITIMACY

The delegitimation of national authority is a process that began among black youth as a consequence of their struggle for constitutionally guaranteed civil rights and for fulfillment of endlessly reiterated promises of economic equality. Despite a continuous stream of pledges, the government repeatedly failed to provide full protection of rights and to implement an effective program of economic improvement for blacks and other poor people. The emergence of black nationalist and revolutionary ideology in the black community is an advanced symptom of the delegitimation of the established political order in the black community.

White activists in the early sixties experienced much of the same disillusionment with governmental authority as a result of their active involvement in the civil rights and antipoverty struggles. The sharpest disillusionment that both black and white activists experienced, however, was failure of the established coalition of liberal and labor organizations to actively press for fundamental change in governmental policy with respect to civil rights, slums, and unemployment.

The Democratic Convention of 1964 may be taken as a critical watershed; had liberal Democrats actively pressed for the incorporation of the civil rights movement into the party at that time, relations of trust might well have been maintained, and both the black movement and the new left may well have continued to operate (albeit uneasily) within the framework of the established two-party system and regular politics. Instead, that Convention confirmed the growing estrangement of young activists from conventional politics. Out of that period emerged black militance and separatism on the one hand and the independent, confrontational radical student movement on the other.

Obviously, the Vietnam war was the second and even deeper disillusionment. Not only did the war reinforce already brewing mistrust and cleavage between young activists and the "old" liberalism, but created a situation in which *all* forms of nonviolent pressure on authority appeared largely futile. *Both* the conventional politics of lobbying, canvassing and voting and the unconventional politics of protest and nonviolent civil disobedience failed to reverse the war policies *even when it became clear that withdrawal from Vietnam had the support of the majority of the electorate.* Moreover, the war had other major delegitimating features: the inequitable and coercive draft, the evident "credibility gap," the fact that it had not been declared a war by Congress, the atrocities and barbarities that flowed from the war strategy, and so forth. Probably no single policy in American history has had as disillusioning an impact on American youth as has the decision to prosecute the war.

But the war and the racial crisis—and the implication of the established political structure in the continuation of both—do not exhaust the conditions that helped the delegitimation process. For example, a crisis in "public happiness" was becoming acute (that is, the apparent incapacity of local and national political institutions to effectively deal with such problems as the deterioration of urban life, pollution of the natural environment, and the decline in the quality of public services). This problem was critically heightened by the fact that the deterioration of public happiness was occurring in the context of a steadily expanding national economy, rising taxes, and public budgets (that is, material resources for dealing with the crisis seemed abundant). Delegitimation was reinforced by the seeming inability of *any* established leadership group to offer a credible way out.

Finally, delegitimation of authority was accelerated because most leaders in government and other positions were failing to articulate the need for a new cultural framework; they seemed to be primarily responsive to those constituencies most attached to the very traditions that numbers of youth found obsolete. Indeed, political leaders within the system who *did* seem to side with the "new" tended to lose their effectiveness (McCarthy, Hickel, and Lindsay, for instance) and some were killed because they did. As I write this, the "establishment" appears to be experiencing a widening and deepening rift on a variety of issues, yet few observers are

predicting that political forces espousing change have much chance
of winning effective power in the near future. Both the traditional-
ism and the divisions of governmental and institutional authority
promote delegitimation, especially when those who most profoundly mistrust the present distribution of power can see little
chance of improving their effective representation.

One of the critical lessons of the past decade, in my view, is
that when significant sectors of the youth are losing trust in established authority, much depends on the actions of established
agencies of reform. In the United States, such established agencies
have included the labor movement, liberal organizations, and
segments of the religious and academic community. These are
groups that have the potential of mobilizing significant numbers of
adults and substantial amounts of money. To the extent that they
can engage in effective mobilization around a credible program
of reform, youths are likely to participate in such an effort and generational conflict and delegitimation of authority will not be evident. The default of these reformist forces has been an important
aspect of the past decade. These forces either tended to resist
the demands of youth and Blacks and continued to support established foreign and domestic policies or gave verbal support to
change but failed to mobilize a semblance of effective power to
back up their rhetoric. Even now when for the first time, a significant section of established liberalism is undertaking rather fundamental criticism of certain policies, there is little evidence of effective mobilization in behalf of a program of change. Simultaneously,
many liberal spokesmen call on youth to "return to the system"
but offer few grounds for so doing.

As the process of mistrust of authority deepens, those who
are actively involved in seeking change feel an increasing need to
resort to tactics of extreme pressure. To the extent that they perceive authority as illegitimate, they come to feel morally bound
to defy it and morally free from the traditional boundaries of the
law. As its legitimacy is overtly challenged, the authority structure
increasingly resorts to naked force to suppress such challenges, and
as a rule, such resort to force further delegitimates those who use
it. Although government is defined as that body which has a monopoly on the means of legitimate violence, the increasing *use* of
such violence by the government to suppress internal opposition is
a clear sign that its legitimacy is eroding.

As the cycle of popular protest and official violence proceeds, protest leaders begin the serious contemplation of "revolution"— that is, they come to define their mission less as a matter of putting pressure on those in power than as one of overthrowing them. In the atmosphere of crisis, delegitimation of authority, protest, and violence, the revolutionists find a widening circle of receptivity. This, indeed, was the situation in the United States by 1970.

Nevertheless, revolutionary rhetoric and action may well be premature or historically out of place. Just as those in power may exaggerate reliability and support of the underlying population, so revolutionists may misjudge the meaning of delegitimation. Despite deep distrust and skepticism of established authority, most people—even those who are quite alienated—retain some hope that peaceful reform is possible and that all-out warfare between the state and its active opposition can be avoided. Indeed, revolutionary rhetoric and guerilla action can have the paradoxical effect of both intensifying mass desire for change *and* heightening mass fears of total breakdown, chaos, and repression. It is clear that throughout the sixties and despite their increasing sympathy for radical change, both black groups and student groups were highly responsive to leaders (Kennedy, McCarthy, and Ralph Nader, for instance) who seemed to promise change through system reform. As long as the process of delegitimation is not total, people retain a residue of hope; as long as this is true, virtually everyone (including many revolutionaries) will resist total commitment to revolutionary solutions.

However, I think that the decline of student protest since Kent State is not attributable primarily to students' hope for progressive reform as an alternative to revolution (although I think this remains a *wish*, if not a hope, for many students). More fundamental, in my view, has been the realization that students, acting as students, can have only limited success in realizing their goals and aspirations with respect to social change. Despite their increased numbers, students represent a small and special minority of the total population; they have few levers on power; and above all, they are isolated.

The isolation of students creates a profound paradox. As we have seen, the segregation of students is the very factor that made the collective consciousness and mass mobilization of youth possible. Furthermore, because universities are key social institutions, campus conflicts have had major historical impact. But the history of student movements everywhere suggests that a point is reached in their development when their isolation and parochialism becomes self-defeating. As students come to define their goals in terms of fundamental reform or revolution, their need to ally themselves with other groups favoring change becomes critical. Nevertheless, such alliances are made problematical by the very characteristics of student life that provide collective strength in the first place—their physical isolation, their privileged freedom from the responsibilities and burdens of adult life, and their speech, dress, tastes, and idealistic impatience.

Second, the student challenge to the university can become self-defeating. In its first phase, that challenge opens up the possibility for basic reform of education, gives students valuable experience in political action, and has profoundly educative effects for many who participate. Campus confrontations, however, are largely unintelligible to many in the outside world who cannot understand the seeming ingratitude of "these pampered kids" for the privileged sanctuaries with which they have been provided. Meanwhile, the authorities learn how to cope with campus disruption, and the limited freedoms on the campus that have facilitated the growth of the movement are called into question. Ultimately, the very existence of the universities seems jeopardized to many faculty and students. Student activists come to see that the political value of campus confrontation is limited or that fundamental university reform cannot occur before general social reform is achieved. Youths who continue to *need* the university (and there are many more who do than will admit it) become increasingly cautious, while others give it up in disgust and drop out.

Third, the student movement is an ambiguous framework for the establishment of personal identity. On the one hand, participation in student protest activity can be enormously liberating and crystallizing. The movement "changes one's life" by freeing many students from the anxieties of individual status-seeking and careerism, by offering alternatives to materialism, by providing opportunities for deeply fraternal and communal relations with others, and by fostering deep commitments to the pursuit of social justice. Few activists, as far as I can tell, return to conventionality after they have been involved with the movement; most find that the movement's values have become deeply internalized as their own. But a student movement, as such, offers very little guidance in determining *concretely* what one should do with one's life after "graduation." There is a timeless quality about the movement; it embodies an assumption that one always will be a student or an ex-student—leading the freelance, experimental, not-tied-down existence of youth. Such timelessness fits well with apocalyptic visions of the future: since nuclear war, fascism, or revolution are imminent (as many activists come to feel they are), one cannot plan one's future anyway. Nevertheless, if a part of you cannot accept the reality of the apocalypse, then the problems of the future become acute. One cannot go "back" to societally programmed identities, but the movement offers little to help the process of going forward.

Thus, *the logic of student movements is that they must transcend themselves if the collective consciousness they express is to survive and realize itself.* Youth must find a way to connect its interests with those of other groups that potentially or actually are in motion for radical change. The students' privileged sanctuary in the university must somehow be transcended. A radicalism relevant to those who are not youth must be created.

I think that if the era of intense campus conflict has come to a pause, this is so because socially concerned students sense the need for such a transcendence but have not yet found the means to achieve it. The organized new left disintegrated into warring factions over precisely the question of how to transcend the limits of student radicalism. Furthermore, it does appear that many new left ideologues have felt disoriented or discredited as a result of their overemphasis of "revolutionary" rhetoric and action and their misjudgment of the imminence of social breakdown.

In short, the era of *campus* confrontation and *student* revolutionism has ended not because it failed, but because it reached the limit of its possibilities. In a real sense, the new left and the student movement succeeded in ways that were hardly imagined by those who founded it. The two social inventions of intellectual youth—the youth counterculture and the student new left—have been crucial in the transformation of the consciousness of an entire generation. By creating new modes of being young, these inventions helped to undermine an already obsolete cultural framework and an already stagnating political order. But, we ought to ask, having performed work of necessary destruction, has the youth revolt created any potentialities for positive transformation?

BIBLIOGRAPHICAL NOTES

1.   The concept of identity has been developed by Erik Erikson. See *Identity: Youth and Crisis* (New York: Norton, 1968). The functions of youth cultures are elaborated in a classic essay by Talcott Parsons, "Age and Sex in the Social Structure of the United States," *American Sociological Review* 7 (1942): 604–614. Mannheim's analysis of generation appears in, "The Problem of Generations," *Essays on the Sociology of Knowledge* (New York: Oxford, 1962).

2.   Some standard works on middle and working class youth cultures prior to 1960 are: James Coleman, *The Adolescent Society* (Glencoe: Free Press, 1961); Albert Cohen, *Delinquent Boys* (Glencoe: Free Press, 1955); James Coleman, "The Adolescent Subculture and Academic Achievement," *American Journal of Sociology* 65 (1960): 337–347; Kenneth Keniston, "Social Change and Youth in America," *Daedalus* (Winter 1962): 145–171; August Hollingshead, *Elmtown's Youth* (New York: Wiley, 1949); Rose Goldsen et al., *What College Students Think* (Princeton, N. J.: Van Nostrand, 1960); and R. Nevitt Sanford (ed.), *The American College* (New York: Wiley, 1962).

3.   The rise of a new bohemianism during the fifties among intellectual youth is documented in Theodore Newcomb et al., *Persistence and Change* (New York: Wiley, 1967); Burton Clark and Martin Trow, "Determinants of college student subculture," Mimeographed (Berkeley, Calif.: Center for the Study of Higher Education, University of California, Berkeley, 1960). The links between the youth culture of the sixties and the "beat" movement of the late fifties are explored in Bruce Cook, *The Beat Generation* (New York: Scribners, 1971). Norman Mailer's definition of the "hip" during the fifties appears in "The White Negro," *Dissent* 4 (Summer 1957): 276–293.

4.   The American tradition of youthful intellectual radical bohemianism is explored in the following: Martin Sklar, "On the Proletarian Revolution and the End of Political-Economic Society," *Radical America* 3 (May–June 1969): 1–41; Richard Flacks, "The Revolt of the Young Intelligentsia," in Rod Aya and Norman Miller, *The New American Revolution* (New York: Free Press,

1971). See, also, David Matza, "Subterranean Traditions of Youth " *The Annals* 338, (November 1961): 102–118.

5.   For a discussion of family origins of radical and alienated students, see Richard Flacks, "The Liberated Generation," *Journal of Social Issues* 23 (1967): 52–75; Kenneth Keniston, *The Uncommitted* (New York: Houghton Mifflin, 1965); Kenneth Keniston, *Young Radicals* (New York: Harcourt, Brace & World, 1968).

6.   Some insight into the origins and development of the sixties rock can be obtained from: Nick Cohn, *Rock from the Beginning* (New York: Pocket Books, 1970); Jerry Hopkins, *The Rock Story* (New York: Signet, 1970); and Paul Williams, *Outlaw Blues* (New York: Pocket Books, 1970).

7.   On the history of the new left and the student movement of the sixties see: James J. O'Brien, *A History of the New Left, 1960–68* (Boston: New England Free Press, n.d.); Massimo Teodori, *The New Left: A Documentary History* (Indianapolis: Bobbs-Merrill, 1969). The section concerning the history of student protest during the sixties is based in part on earlier work of mine incorporated into Jerome Skolnick, *The Politics of Protest* (New York: Ballantine Books, 1969), pp. 87–109.

8.   The spread of student protest is reported and discussed in *The Report of the President's Commission on Campus Unrest* (Washington, D. C.: U. S. Government Printing Office, 1970). This report is a reasonably good summary of social science thinking on the causes and extent of student protest and contains a very good bibliography on the subject. Some other recent material of importance on the history, development, and comparative analysis of student protest may be found in: Philip Altbach and Robert S. Laufer (eds.), "Students Protest," *The Annals* 395 (May 1971) whole issue.

5

BEYOND THE YOUTH REVOLT: SOME POSSIBILITIES FOR THE SEVENTIES

The most obvious effect of the youth revolt has been a redefinition of the meaning of youth in American society. Youth has become not only a socially defined stage in the life cycle of the individual but also a clearly differentiated social category. People who identify themselves with this category now do so in terms of distinctive modes of dress, speech, and demeanor and in terms of distinctive tastes and styles in the arts and other means of self-expression. At a deeper level, members of this social category have come to share distinctive mores and values—which stand in self-conscious opposition to those that prevail officially or that adults of many type regard as legitimate.

But most self-conscious youths do not intend their social impact to be restricted to a redefinition of the meaning of youth. At a minimum, the ambition of the counterculture is to create a new way of life that will serve as a viable alternative to those options that have become established in American culture; most counterculturalists, however, hope that in time, their values will *prevail* and *supplant* conventional values. At a minimum, the ambition of student revolutionists is to disrupt and frustrate American imperialism and militarism; most new leftists, however, hope to participate in a thoroughgoing transformation of the American economic and political order.

As I have tried to demonstrate, realization of such revolutionary ambitions requires transcendence of the youth consciousness, youth culture, and generational revolt. A counterculture is not a cultural alternative until it can embody a way of life that will be appropriate to an individual throughout his life cycle. A political movement can tranform society only when it legitimately speaks for the interests and aspirations of the people as a whole.

One way to understand possible developments in the next few years, then, is to work out the various possible individual and collective means that the present generation of youth might employ to transform the society. In making such projections, we are constrained in at least two ways. First, it seems crucial to build such predictions out of the stirrings already evident in the present. Second, it is necessary to try to keep in mind the social conditions that will provide the soil for whatever new developments are to occur. Such conditions include such matters as changes in the age distribution of the population, changes in the labor market and related economic factors, possible efforts by the authority structure and other established institutions to exploit, manipulate, suppress, and incorporate new developments, and the like.

There are two crucial trends that I want to highlight at the outset—two fundamental changes in socioeconomic context that, it seems to me, already distinguished the seventies from the sixties. *First,* there will be a significant increase in the number of young adults age 2 to 35 during this decade. In 1970 there were 40 million persons in this category; by 1975, there will be 50 million persons plus an additional 10 million youths between 18 and 21 years. This means that persons born since the beginning of World War II will represent well over 40 percent of the electorate by 1975. As we shall see, this situation opens up possibilities for changes in American politics not previously available.

Second, there is now, for the first time, a serious problem of unemployment and economic insecurity for college graduates. This situation is partly a result of the (apparently) temporary economic recession of the late sixties and early seventies, but the tightening job market for the educated may be the result of deeper, more chronic problems—problems that will not be dissolved by a new period of boom. A very substantial portion of the unemployment problem for the educated is attributable to restrictions in government budgets.

As I pointed out in Chapter 3, the system of higher education was expanded to provide manpower for activities that were largely funded by government: research and development, education, and social services. Cutbacks in government spending for military research and development, for public education, higher education and for antipoverty programs, have transformed the job situation for college graduates. On the one hand, many scientists and technicians with advanced degrees are unemployed because of defense cutbacks. On the other hand, recent college graduates and PhDs who enter fields such as teaching confront a tight job market because of government freezes on expenditures for education at all levels. If present budgetary criteria for education are continued, nearly 50 percent of those trained as teachers might well be unable to enter their chosen field. Simultaneously, graduate schools have begun to limit enrollments because of the declining market for those with graduate degrees. Professional schools are overwhelmed by applications. The ratio of unemployed college youths is higher than the national average; students and graduates are competing with traditional workers for blue-collar work. After twenty-five years of unparalleled opportunity for the highly educated and prosperity for the educational establishment (especially universities), economic insecurity suddenly has become a reality. How permanent this situation is cannot be known, for it is very largely dependent on conscious political decision rather than on impersonal market forces. Nevertheless, the change in economic circumstances of the educated is sure to have an effect on the behavior and perspectives of those it affects. There is a paradox involved here. On the one hand, much of the search for cultural alternatives has been rooted in affluence and economic security. If college students face economic insecurity, will they become more cautious? On the other hand, the radicalization of youth in other societies has almost always been associated with significant unemployment among the college educated. Does the rise of unemployment for the educated portend further radicalization?

Thus, as we try to assess the next developments for the generation of the sixties, we need to keep in mind that in two respects, the world that generation is graduating into is significantly different from the one they have experienced and been shaped by. First, the new young adults will have a numerical potential without previous parallel; second, that they will attain the affluence and material security of their youth is considerably less certain than they have been led to believe.

In the discussion that follows I want to concentrate first on spelling out what seem to be the most important developments, trends, and potentialities that foster the aims and values of the youth revolt. There is a "revolutionary" logic to the youth revolt, and we will consider some of the factors that promote the fulfillment of that logic. (Here, I use the word revolution to connote fundamental qualitative change in the social, political and cultural system—change toward a new order organized around new values and institutional arrangements—change not deliberately promoted and planned by those who now hold decisive power.) Finally, I want to suggest some factors that may spell the dissolution rather than the expansion of the new consciousness.

TRENDS FAVORABLE TO REVOLUTIONARY LOGIC

The Spread of New Consciousness to Nonstudent Youth

By the late sixties, it was already evident that the new youth culture was not restricted to students and middle class youth. As I pointed out in Chapter 4, acceptance of the new music, long hair, and drugs very rapidly spread to high schools. By the end of the decade, many elements of the new culture had penetrated to locales that previously had been intensely hostile—the military bases and the factories. More important, not only drugs, music, and hair were adopted by soldiers and young workers, but also overt expression of hostility toward the government and other established authority, open display of alienation, and a considerable sense of solidarity with other sectors of youth.

This was particularly evident in the military. The use of marijuana and hard drugs on bases at home and in Vietnam had become an open and serious problem by 1971. Military regulations governing appearance were liberalized in response to the increased flouting of rules governing hair by both black and white personnel. More significant was the open organization of opposition to the war and in behalf of GI rights that became evident. A network of underground newspapers flourished. GIs increasingly took part in overt protest activity. By the spring of 1971, Vietnam veterans and GIs in general had become the catalytic force in the antiwar movement. These protesters replaced students as the most active, articulate and effectively militant group. Distinctions of attitude, sentiment, and behavior between the men in uniform and the campus "hippies," which Presidents Johnson and Nixon had been fond of making, had very largely disappeared.

The reasons for the spread of the youth revolt to the military are not hard to discern. The morale of a conscript army is perhaps always somewhat shaky, but maintaining the morale of an army that is fighting a conflict that is not even properly termed a war is impossible. This is especially so when the President espouses a goal of disengagement. The indignity and sacrifice inherent in military life were, by the end of the decade, hardly justified by even vague patriotic appeals. Under these circumstances, overt acts of protest and resistance by a few highly committed men were able to mobilize the sympathy, support, and emulation of ever widening numbers of others. To the extent that GIs were restricted to symbolic action, it was natural that they would adopt the very symbols of defiance that other youth had already invented.

For an unknown but probably large number of GIs, the military experience, combined with new consciousness, had a "resocializing" impact comparable to that experienced by many students. Many were leaving the army with a profound mistrust of government authority and deep feelings of discontent with the society they were reentering. These feelings were undoubtedly intensified by the uncommonly high rate of unemployment of Vietnam veterans. Moreover, the mood of questioning of and restlessness with official values and established policies had penetrated even the military elite. Service academy graduates were active in the antiwar protest; dissent was evident even at West Point.

Throughout the sixties, most observers expected that veterans of Vietnam would constitute a new source of energy for patriotism and bitterness at those who opposed the war effort. By the early seventies, however, it appeared more likely that the most active of the returning vets would be those who were angered by the men and policies that had promulgated the war in the first place and that the organized political energies of returning vets would fuse with the radicalism of students.

Meanwhile, a less dramatic but comparable development among young workers was becoming evident. Partly, this was because of an influx of students and veterans into the blue-collar labor force, because of the intensifying militance of black workers, and because of general processes of cultural diffusion that have affected other young people. In any case, by the early seventies long hair could be seen sprouting from under an increasing number of hard hats, union officials were taking note of the increased militance of young members, and some unions were beginning to take an active part in the antiwar movement. Increasingly, drug use on the job was being described as a serious and growing problem. Undoubtedly, many young white workers were polarizing to the political right—for instance, supporting George Wallace—but the potential for a parallel emergence of young worker leftism seemed to be increasing. The possibilities for a sharing of consciousness between students and working youth would, of course, be greatly enhanced if students were to consciously attempt to bring this about. Some efforts at such organization were, in fact, occurring by the end of the sixties.

The "Territorialization" of the Youth Culture

Bohemian subcultures have always gravitated to specific geographic locales—usually, to urban neighborhoods—where the life style could be maintained in a community of like-minded people. For several years, a similar concentration of the new bohemians of the sixties has been evident—in the East Village, Berkeley, Haight-Ashbury, and a few other locales.

By the early seventies, however, the bohemian enclave was more aptly described as a "youth ghetto," attracting not simply a few artists and writers and an exotic cultural fringe, but young people of many social strata who shared a common desire for a new life style and a common interest in the emerging counterculture. These newer communities were, therefore, considerably younger, considerably larger, and more heterogeneous than were the traditional ones. Since much of their commonality revolved around illegal drug use and militant protest, the youth settlements, like urban ghettoes, experienced intense police surveillance and harassment and the inevitable riots that accompany such police occupation. They resembled black ghettoes (albeit in much milder form) in that they typically experienced considerable economic exploitation at the hands of landlords, storekeepers, and other commercial interests and had virtually no sources of political power to counter such exploitation and repression. By the early seventies, there was an impressive number of youth ghettoes. They had emerged in every large city and university town, and particularly in the latter, their populations included both "dropouts" and more socially integrated students. Obviously, many inhabitants were highly transient "street-people," but many others were more permanently established and employed young adults.

As is the case in all highly transient locales, youth ghettoes exhibited many of the classic symptoms of anomie and social disorganization: high rates of violent crime, suicide, and drug addiction; the visible presence of severely strung-out and dislocated persons; and the flourishing of exotic varieties of mysticism and religious cults. Police harassment intensified widespread feelings of paranoia and mutual mistrust, but the symbols and sentiments of the youth culture provided a basis for solidarity and consensus in these communities.

Typically, after an intense experience of confrontation with the police, feelings of solidarity crystallized around broad community movements for self-determination and the development of ongoing "counter institutions." By the early seventies, many youth ghettoes had become scenes of intensive institutional experimentation as activists sought to put into practice the values embodied by the counterculture and the new left. Food co-ops, tenant organizations, credit unions, underground media, childcare centers, block organizations, organic gardens, people's parks, ecology centers, free schools, media collectives, book stores, free clinics, and therapeutic networks—these were the types of institution that began to merge. They were designed to enable the community to provide itself with needed services, to compete with established commercial interests, to provide alternatives to conventional institutional arrangements, and to test the possibilities for cooperative modes of living that were noncapitalist and nonbureaucratic.

Underneath the community counterinstitutions, new patterns of interpersonal relations were being tried in the youth ghettoes. There was a rapid growth of "collective" living arrangements: self-conscious efforts by small groups composed of both sexes to combine resources and share household responsibilities, often with the explicit aim of finding alternatives to conventional room-mate and nuclear family living patterns. Often, such collectives shared a common public project. Not only were they working on building a household, but also collectively putting out a newspaper, operating a free school, doing political organizing, or running a legal defense center. Nevertheless, many collectives were simply struggling with the task of living together in communal fashion. By the early seventies, there was a widespread yearning among self-conscious youth for concrete ways to implement the vision of a "humanistic life style." Thus, the collectives and other interpersonal experiments have become efforts to establish "honest," "authentic" sexual relationships and friendships, to struggle with the problem of sexual equality on a face-to-face level, and to see whether the conventional nuclear family-consumerist way of living and childrearing can be replaced by a life style less dependent on possession, security, and parents.

Thus, the development of community consciousness in youth ghettoes has created the opportunity for institutional experiment in accordance with the values embodied by the youth revolt. It has also created a new basis for political consciousness. Youth ghetto inhabitants have begun to sense that their geographical concentration provides them with certain kinds of potential political power. In large part, this is the power of mass mobilization, protest and direct action. But the increasing number of young adults in the youth ghettoes combined now with the 18 year old vote has led to renewed interest in the formal political system, in the possibilities inherent in a youth bloc vote, and of thereby exercising some decisive direct influence in the government of the local community. Already, this political mobilization has produced significant bloc voting—even before passage of the 18 year old voting amendment.

The most dramatic case thus far is that of Berkeley, where a radical coalition of youths and blacks succeeded in electing a slate of candidates to the Berkeley city council. In Isla Vista, the youth ghetto adjacent to the University of California, Santa Barbara, a pattern of bloc voting has begun to have an impact on local politics.

Assuming that energy continues to be mobilized for the internal development of youth communities, my feeling is that they offer considerable promise as one route for institutionalizing and transcending the youth revolt. First, the youth ghetto could become a major testing ground for the implementation of cultural transformation—through the development of counterinstitutions and new social relations. To the extent that such new life styles can be seen to "work"—that is to provide more satisfying, rational, life-enhancing means to solving critical personal and social problems—they are likely to influence the consciousness of many in the outside world. Probably, such youth communities would become magnets for increasing numbers of young adults—as places to settle that would be better than conventional urban and suburban areas.

Most important, the youth community could serve (indeed does serve) a major educational and resocializing function—providing those who move out of it into more conventional environments both the desire and the skill to attempt to build and organize counterinstitutions in the "straight" world.

Moreover, the youth communities can play a critical and direct political role. There is no question, for example, that should 18 year olds be permitted to vote where they live, local politicians will have to confront the existence of a substantial new voting bloc with an increasingly clear sense of political direction. One can predict with great assurance that as a result, new styles of political opportunism and demagoguery will be invented by established politicians either to court the youth vote or build opposition to it. What is less predictable is whether an independent political force along the lines begun in Berkeley, initiated by youths themselves, will emerge out of the youth ghettoes. My own feeling is that such an indigenous radical politics could develop real strength based in the youth communities and could have significant local impact if it were able to join in coalition with other groups—black and brown people, for example—that are searching for political alternatives. I will develop this theme below.

There is a further implication of the territorialization of youth culture. To the extent that the sentiments and life styles associated with youth are institutionalized, "youth" begins to lose its age-specific character. The creation of "jobs" in counterinstitutions and the sharing of economic and childrearing responsibilities in col-

lectives suggest means to permanently and viably refuse adult roles
as they are currently defined in our culture. Another way of stating
this is to argue that these developments permit at least some youth
to fulfill the identities they have achieved as youth in biological
adulthood—a circumstance that is largely frustrated by the conventional culture except for those of independent wealth or the
talent to make a life within the bohemian tradition.

If the impulse to preserve a youthful identity leads some
to settle within the framework of youth ghettoes, it leads an increasing number of others to a more thoroughgoing withdrawal
from city, suburb, and industrial civilization. The youth culture is
becoming territorialized by way of rural communes and households
established in an effort to live off the land, to live cooperatively,
to exist in maximum self-sufficiency and, hopefully, free from the
pressures of competitive work, police, pollution, crowds, and the
corruptions of technological affluence.

It is too soon to tell whether migration to the countryside
constitutes a long-term trend—too early to know whether city-bred
types can make it on the land in any permanent way and find
satisfaction in doing so. If such migration were to become significant, it would no doubt weaken the direct political impact that
the rising youth constituency might have, particularly if such migration drained off from the urban centers those who would be among
the more creatively discontented within them. Indeed, dispersion
of potentially vanguard youth in the countryside might well undermine the very conditions of concentration that have permitted the
youth culture to develop and youth to be mobilized. On the other
hand, the new communards could well argue that the successful
construction of a new way of life in the country might be a crucial
demonstration of the irrationality of established culture, and consequently a more potent political achievement than are more direct
forms of political action. Thus, the rural commune movement
shares with the community development movement a common desire to live out the values of the youth revolt, to carry out in
practice a cultural revolution. Whether these two efforts are com-
plementary or mutually exclusive remains to be seen. In any case,
they represent important signs that the youth culture is being institutionalized and, hence, becoming an established way of life.
A key question in the coming decade is likely to be whether the

effort to construct alternatives to prevailing patterns of urban and suburban life and to the middle class nuclear family household does indeed represent the dominant mode of living for the future or is merely a struggle to survive on the part of those who cannot accept their place in techno-corporate civilization.

The Radicalization of "Educated Labor"

Youth enclaves and rural communes are expressions of those youth who are resisting entrance into the occupations and careers for which they have been programmed. Rather than refuse such roles, other youth have begun to accept them, consciously attempting to remake them in terms of the moral and political perspectives embodied by the student movement. Thus, in the past few years, in virtually every professional field, self-conscious groupings of young practitioners who are organized to challenge the established assumptions, practices, and leaderships of their fields have emerged. In the legal and health professions, for instance, youthful elements are actively creating what might be called a "socialized" practice, in which the services of these professions can be delivered to clients on an egalitarian basis, and the status and power hierarchies within the professions are fundamentally altered. Similar developments are evident within such fields as social work, urban planning, sociology, psychology, history, anthropology, and the academic profession as a whole. Essentially what is being demanded is that professional practice be reorganized so that the needs of the underprivileged for services will be met, that emphasis on status competition and material success within the professions be replaced by a social ethic, that scholars be free to undertake radical criticism of established institutions and to propose revolutionary alternatives, and that the shaping of the professions and disciplines by corporate and governmental priorities and status quo values be replaced by essentially antiestablishment and postcapitalist modes of professional work.

Out of this ferment, new sets of organizations, new institutions, and new intellectual positions and activities are emerging. Young medical professionals establish free clinics and organize to challenge the conservative policies of the AMA and the inegalitarian practices of major hospitals. Young lawyers establish legal centers in urban ghettoes, use their skills in class-action suits in behalf of consumers, and seek to expose the inequities and injustices built into the routine operations of the legal system. Young historians develop "revisionist" interpretations of the meaning of American history, young sociologists work on social analyses deriving from the theoretical perspectives of the new left, and young psychologists are attracted to "humanistic" models of man and therapeutic practice. The activities of the young radical professionals force fundamental reexaminations of the structure of the professions, percolate back into the universities and are likely to have an increasingly disruptive effect on the structural and ideological framework of the American intellectual-scientific-professional apparatus.

It is already possible to glimpse some of the potentialities of this "radicals-in-the-professions" movement.

A fundamental remaking of the identity of professionals is implied by these movements. The attack on professional elitism leads to an effort to make the knowledge and skills of the professional elites accessible to people without professional education and formal credentials—to break down the barriers between professional and client, between professional and his "aides," to create a *community* of people who can participate more equally in the achievement of health, in the formulation of education, in the defense of their rights, and in the planning of their environments. In more concrete terms, the egalitarian movement in these "professional fields" seeks to abolish racism and sexism in recruitment to and in the structure of the fields, to open up new modes of training for work in these fields, to provide free services and to educate clients rather than to mystify them, to enable nonprofessionals to participate actively in the offering of services, and so forth. Increasing numbers of young doctors and lawyers live and work in communal fashion, at a subsistence level—in part to free themselves from dependence on established institutions, in part to free themselves from the deeply ingrained individualism that is fostered by professional aspirations and training.

Out of these movements increasingly explicit programs for fundamental social reform are emerging. For example, the radical health movement is devoting increasing energy to the formulation of concrete proposals for the transformation of the "health system" —proposals that can become politically potent as demands of community organizations. A similar process is evident in such diverse areas as consumer rights, education, the governance of corporations, pollution, social welfare, criminal justice, and penology. In short, at just the time that the "Establishment" seems to be losing the capacity to formulate solutions to an intensifying array of social crises, a new energy for basic social reform can be glimpsed in the organizations and collectives of young radical professionals. In all cases, the new visions entail not primarily more government subsidy for social services (the basic theme of past reform movements), but a fundamental dismantling of established bureaucracies and existing modes of control of such services.

If the youth revolt has, up to now, been charged with a failure to propose concrete alternatives, such charges will be less and less relevant as the new radicalism in the professions develops. But, unlike some prophets of the "greening" of American institutions, I cannot see that the new identities and visions will come to dominate the professions simply because a new generation "takes over" and supplants the old. The visions embodied in the new generation of professionals require a *qualitative* transformation in the *meaning* of such "services" as medicine, education, legal defense, social work, planning, and the like. These visions, in other words, are in *fundamental* conflict with established institutions and political practices and cannot be implemented simply by having "groovier" men and women running the Establishment.

What is likely, then, is a considerable period of conflict and confrontation within the institutions into which the new generation is now graduating.

In a sense, the spirit of the student movement and the campus revolt is being carried into the medical complex, the law office, the government bureau, the newspaper office, the research center, the professional convention, and the faculty meeting. Already, even the tactics of student protest are popping up in these places, and new forms of protest and confrontation are being developed.

It is plausible to conjecture that the spread of the campus revolt into the professions and intellectual workplaces prefigures the emergence of a new class consciousness among those engaged in what might be called "educated labor." This consciousness focuses around demands that are much more far reaching and less easy to accommodate than those traditionally raised by labor unions (although the unionization of "professionals" is clearly on the agenda). Given the rapidly increasing numerical size of the professional and technical workforce and its increasingly strategic role in the operation of the political economy, many radical theorists have come to argue that this class has the potential of fulfilling the revolutionary role which Marx expected for the industrial proletariat. Whether or not this is true, and there are many reasons to qualify such an argument, there seems little question that the organization of this occupational group around political, social, and cultural issues and for the purpose of transforming its social functions would have major implications for the future development of American society. Such organization, it seems to me, is both logically and psychologically derivable from the student revolt.

Women's Liberation and the Sex Role Revolt

Another logical outcome of the youth revolt has been the rapid emergence of the women's liberation movement. The new women's movement can be viewed as partly an outgrowth of the youth movement for several reasons. On the one hand, the counterculture's general assault on established values and the student movement's efforts to legitimate *all* protest by subordinate groups helped create the climate, the ideological framework, the experience, and the tactics that enabled young, primarily college-educated women to organize in their own interest. But the youth culture and the new left catalyzed women's liberation in another, negative, sense—as young women found the need to organize *against* what they came to realize was the male-centeredness of the youth movement.

As a result of the feminist critique of the new left and the youth culture, we can now see that one of the most serious limitations of both the movement and the counterculture was that they were dominated by young men and served male needs.

The youth culture of the sixties, in fact, can be interpreted as almost entirely an expression of the inability of certain types of *male* youth to accept the conventional definitions of the *male* role. A great deal of the symbolism and activity of the youth culture reflected the efforts of males to find cultural alternatives for themselves with respect both to work and to other aspects of identity. But the new symbols and values failed to reflect any significant change of feeling or practice with respect to the treatment of women and much of the content and style of the new music was even more explicitly exploitative and callous toward women than was anything found in straight pop culture. In fact, the new sexual morality made women even more vulnerable to sexual exploitation than traditional standards had—although, presumably, they were now permitted to obtain pleasure as well as to give it.

The new left, although less explicitly masculine in the issues it addressed, was dominated by male organizational and intellectual leadership. On the whole, women were relegated to clerical and menial tasks and excluded from active participation in political debate and leadership—presumably because of a variety of subtle and unconscious means of intimidation and manipulation employed by the highly articulate male leaders of the movement. As the movement became more militant, many males found it an excellent arena for competitive displays of virility, toughness, and physical courage—a situation that undoubtedly played a role in shaping the tactical direction that the movement took in the late sixties.

Thus, women's liberation may be interpreted as an expression by young women who, as a result of their participation in the youth revolt, had developed a new sense of their rights and an awareness of their oppression. These women considered that not only was the youth revolt irrelevant to their interests, but it offered males a new cultural pattern by which they could dominate women.

Thus, the liberation movement has been largely separatist—it is fiercely independent of male-dominated radicalisms and maintains a barrage of biting criticism of them. In a short time, the women's movement has "reached" women of many ages and from diverse strata, many of whom had been relatively unaffected by the movements of the sixties. A new framework of social and cultural criticism and analysis has emerged—from the feminist point of view.

In certain respects, the women's liberation consciousness embodies an assault on established culture that is more penetrating and fundamental than that of the counterculture. This is not the place for me to develop that point in any detail. Let me indicate, however, what I think are central issues that the women's movement has begun to dramatize—issues whose settlement would be quite decisive for the future of our civilization.

For instance, is the link between sex and power, both within the family and in the larger society, at the core of motives to dominate, compete with, and subjugate fellow humans? Is it plausible that authentically egalitarian relations between the sexes would enhance the psychological capacity of individuals to love, cooperate, and share? Is role differentiation in the middle class nuclear family—that is, masculine monopoly on occupational status and feminine monopoly on consumership—a primary mechanism for sustaining the "rat-race"? Would a system based on the pursuit of profit and competitive individualism be able to sustain itself if sexual inequality were abolished? Is it plausible that the privatized, anxiety-ridden status-seeking that seems to be the motivational energy for middle class economic behavior could be alleviated if the nuclear family ceased to be the principal unit of private consumption and if women had full equality in the labor market? These are some of the basic questions that the women's liberation movement raises for the central values of capitalist culture.

Clearly, the consciousness reflected in such questions is congruent with the impulses toward collective living, new modes of child care, and male rejection of careerism that derive from the counterculture. Thus, the new feminism, even though it is a rebellion against the sexism of the youth revolt, ultimately reinforces and intensifies the effort to construct an alternative way of life that the youth revolt expressed. In particular, it channels countercultural energy most particularly in the direction of redefining the family and the household and complements and deepens the masculine search for alternatives to conventional careers.

It is not yet clear that women have found the most effective forms for carrying through the implications of this changing consciousness. To the extent, however, that they can, the implications for the culture are far reaching. Not only does the women's movement imply basic change in sexuality, relations between the sexes, and the status of women, but also embodies the potentiality for change in such cultural dimensions as the resort to violence, the meaning of work, and the structure of character.

A Return to Politics?

One of the sources of radical political and cultural energy in the sixties was failure of the political system to effectively represent the aspirations and demands that were coming to the fore on college campuses and in urban ghettoes. As we have seen, failure of established liberalism to organize effective support for the civil rights movement in 1964 and of the Democratic party to accept the demands of the antiwar movement in 1968 were important turning points—events that intensified and accelerated the radicalization of young people. The fact that youths and blacks felt excluded from an effective voice in normal politics led inevitably to support for militant, extralegal tactics and to increasing interest in the idea of revolution. Moreover, the fact that politics did not "work" led many to channel their energies into the construction of the counterculture and counterinstitutions rather than to rely on governmental processes to effect basic change. Finally, the war, and the larger crisis of which it was a part, reinforced and deepened fundamental mistrust of political authority and of the political process as a whole.

From a sociological point of view, such a redirection of energy seems right as a way to initiate deep social change. The implicit insight of the youth movement—that social transformation cannot be brought about by legislatively enacted reform but must begin with the transformation of social relations and culture—marks an important advance in the history of social movements in America. Despite the power of the state, the political process clearly is more a reflector than an initiator of basic social change.

Nevertheless, to assume that basic change can occur outside the political system is a gross error. In the first place, the authorities have considerable power to block change by means of the enormous arsenal of coercive and repressive measures they command. On the other hand, governmental practices can facilitate change—through verbal support, through the allocation of resources, or simply through refusal to intervene in the face of social conflict.

Second, the demands of social movements must eventually be reflected in new policies, new laws, or a restructuring of the political system as a whole if demands are to be achieved. Movements for basic change must stay free of the entanglements of regular politics if they are to work changes in popular consciousness, but the new consciousness that is thus created must gain political power if the movement is to survive (and not be repressed) and if its practical goals are to be realized. That seems to be one of the basic dilemmas of all movements that seek basic change in the social order, especially in societies that have a semblance of formal democracy in government.

As I write this there are few signs that radical political activists who have eschewed electoral activity for several years are now ready to return to such a strategy. But there *are* straws in the wind: most dramatic and significant, in the Berkeley city elections in the Spring of 1971, when young white radicals combined forces with a slate of left-oriented blacks and succeeded in electing three council members.

The Berkeley elections coincided with important changes in the age composition of the electorate. The most obvious change was that passage of the Twenty-Sixth Amendment in 1971 granted voting rights to those 18 years and older. This amendment added some 12 million youths to the potential electorate, and early reports on their party registration suggested a marked departure from the Republican party on the part of registrants. Less discussed, but equally significant is the increase in the proportion of voters under 25—post-school age young adults whose ranks will exceed 1968 figures by 20 percent in 1972 and by another 20 percent in 1976—a total increase of 40 percent. By 1972 election time, well over 45 million voters who were "youth" during the sixties and seventies will be eligible to vote. This figure will increase to well over 60 million by 1976 (nearly 45 percent of the total electorate).

This huge potential constituency is extremely diverse. Indeed, many political analysts argue that the young voter will have little effect on American politics. Basing their arguments on past experience, they predict that young voters will behave in much the same way as their parents have, voting according to the party preferences of their parents and becoming more conservative with age. Moreover, they argue that traditionally, the rate of young voters who participate in elections is low because they are politically indifferent, because they are less stable in their residence than older voters are, and because electoral uninvolvement is likely to be intensified by the increased alienation of youth from the electoral process.

Such projections of past voting behavior on to the newly enfranchised youth and young adult population may be extremely shortsighted. First, residency requirements have been somewhat eased, thus removing some of the barriers to voting faced by young adults in the past.

Second, there is a consciousness among the young that they do constitute a potentially powerful constituency—a consciousness most intense among those who are or have been in college. This consciousness is in part a consequence of the youth culture and the consequent mutual identification of young people. It was strongly reinforced by the McCarthy campaign in 1968 and by the Berkeley elections in 1971. It is continuously further reinforced by the media and by politicians who are eager to base their power on such a newly available mass of voters (for instance, Allard Lowenstein).

Third, school youth are probably the most readily mobilized group in the whole society for political campaigns since they can be easily reached and have the time and energy for campaign activity.

Finally, and perhaps of greatest significance, there is a possibility that students and other youth, voting as a bloc, can have a *decisive* voice in many towns and districts where they constitute majorities, sizable minorities, or swing votes. Such local power for youth-student blocs is, however, now frustrated by residency rules excluding students from voting where they attend school; on the other hand, some states have already ruled in favor of student residency, and the matter is being widely contested in the courts. Certainly, those politicians (mostly Democrats in Republican-controlled localities) who have an interest in encouraging youth to vote will be pressing for change in residency policies. In any case, the potential decisiveness of the youth vote is likely to increase the interest of young people in the electoral process.

Assuming, then, the existence of an increasingly self-conscious constituency of young voters, which is strongly disaffected from traditional political styles and attracted to reform-oriented politics, some important changes in American politics seem likely.

Professional politicians will seek youth support. This has

been happening with increasing frequency in recent years, most visibly in the McCarthy primary campaign in 1968, but also in a number of congressional races. Until now, however, youth were sought more for their campaign energy than for their voting support. Moreover, the Vietnam war created a set of simple, stark issues that would very predictably generate the support of politically interested young people. A long-term problem for professional politicians is to determine bases of appeal to youth, apart from the war issue, that can crystallize support (without at the same time alienating potential supporters in other constituencies). Obviously, some politicians will opt for "style," some for "issues"; some may be able to combine both; and some will attempt to exploit the possibilities of "backlash" against the young.

In the next few years, we are likely to see a fascinating array of efforts to find the appropriate symbolism, style, and rhetoric to appeal to young voters. Middle-aged men will adopt elements of youthful costuming and jargon. A breed of young politician will emerge—a breed who will strive to find the right combination of "hipness" and maturity to win. Political "experts" will debate whether youth want candidates who act like youth or mature politicians who can communicate. Commentators will pontificate over the relative merits of "style" and "substance," and all of us will have difficulty distinguishing the phony and the sincere.

On the whole, it seems plausible that the rhetoric and style of mainstream American politics will shift toward reform, liberalism, and change (although a new type of rear guard politician will successfully exploit the fears of those who feel threatened by the new symbols). Nevertheless, changes going deeper than style are entirely possible. Already, candidates for the presidency in both parties have emerged who intend to appeal to the youth vote on the basis of substantive issues and are opposed by the established machinery of their parties. The Democratic Convention of 1972 promises to witness an intense battle over candidates, policies, and control of the party—a battle that will be made more likely if the youth-oriented candidates have success in primary races and in garnering delegates.

Simultaneously, there is an interest among certain established political elements in creating a new party of the left—an interest stimulated by the existence of the potential youth vote. A splintering of the Democratic party or the emergence of a new liberal party with Establishment backing is thus made possible by the emergence of the young voter. These would certainly be important occurrences. Their likelihood depends on the actual potency of the youth vote, the degree of resistance to change on the part of those who now control the Democratic party, and on the degree to which the youth-oriented politicians are serious in pressing their professed aims.

One could speculate indefinitely about the possible implications of the youth vote on the behavior of professionl politicians and the alignment of the parties. My own feeling is that the implications are in fact considerable, but the meaning of such shifting for the future of the larger society is relatively limited. If the main political outcome of the youth revolt is the creation of a youth constituency as a new base for professional politicians, the consequences for major reform will be relatively insubstantial. Transformation of the young rebel into the young voter will mean that political initiative in society will have passed back from those who oppose authority to those who exercise it. As long as professional politicians—whether they are youthful or mature, honest or phony—can manipulate a passive constituency of youth, the best one can expect is an atmosphere that is relatively permissive rather than repressive. Certainly a situation in which the fundamental aspirations of the youth revolt will be effectively voiced or acted upon by those in power cannot be expected.

The Berkeley case suggests an additional possibility. That is, young radicals will themselves take political initiative, entering the political arena directly on the basis of radical programs independent of established professional politicians. The same constituency that is potentially available to provide passive support to a new breed of liberal politician is also available for support of a more radical coalition interested in using the electoral process to further demands rather than careers. The fact that students, street youth, and hip young adults can constitute a decisive constituency in a considerable number of locales is likely to lead cadres of the radical movement toward an electoral strategy in such communities. Such a strategy will improve its chances of success if the student-youth constituency can be linked locally with substantial constituencies in black, brown, and white working class communities.

What the program of such local radical political alliances might consist of is not yet obvious. Nevertheless, certain principles are likely to sharply distinguish the independent radical politicoes from the reform politicians with whom they may be in competition. First, the radicals will probably take a sharply critical stance toward "law and order" and seek through races for election to posts such as sheriff, district attorney, and city attorney basic changes in the administration of justice: community control of the police, nonviolent means to maintain order, an authentically representative jury system, and a great variety of related reforms in the operation of the police, the courts, and other agencies.

Second, radicals are likely to focus their attacks on the activities of large corporations—tying concerns about pollution, consumer protection, exploitation of workers, taxes, and unemployment to the operation of the profit system and the power of the corporations to shape governmental policy. Thus, the radical alliances are likely to experiment with a renewal of socialist ideology and with efforts to focus political debate on the need to find an alternative to corporate capitalism rather than to propose reforms to improve the functioning of the system.

Finally, radicals can be expected to present candidates who do not fit the mold of the professional politician—candidates who have demonstrated capacities for leadership, not as lawyers, businessmen, or celebrities, but as activists in grass-roots movements.

In addition to such local activity based in youth ghetto areas, it seems likely that some segments of American radicalism will try to create a national political party. The history of radical third parties in America suggests that they are doomed to the status of splinter groups, that they fail to gather a sizable following, and that they fade quickly. To the extent that the Democratic party continues to be able to absorb the support of the poor, the ethnic minorities, labor, and reformers, any new national party of the left seems likely to share the fate of its predecessors. On the other hand, a significant split in the Democratic party, involving efforts to start a new national party on the part of reform-oriented professional politicians, might provide the basis for a viable third-party movement on the national level. Radicals would then face the dilemma of whether to ally themselves with a new party of liberal reform (thereby compromising more revolutionary goals) or maintain their independence. At this early date, the best hope for constructing an effective radical political movement would seem to lie in developing grass-roots radical-populist-socialist political organizations in the *localities* where radical sentiments are strongest rather than in devoting energy primarily to organizing a *national* party of the left.

I have dwelled this long on rather airy political speculation, not because I imagine myself a pundit, but in order to get you to think about the possible effects that the transformation of the American electorate could have on the style, tone, content, and organization of American politics. Politicians, experts, and ordinary citizens alike have been operating for several decades on a set of assumptions about the way American politics works—assumptions about the inevitability of the two-party system, about the permanence of local political machines, about the irrelevance of political campaigns to real issues, and so forth. The rise of the youth voter suggests that these assumptions are shortly to become obsolete and that the nature of party politics nationally and locally is going to be radically changed during the seventies.

Movements of the sixties discovered that it was virtually impossible to make change through normal political activity but that it was entirely possible to affect the course of history through direct action, social experiment, and cultural expression. By the beginning of the seventies, however, it had become clear that without political expression, social movements remain isolated from potential allies, are blocked in achieving their aims, and may suffer repression by those in power. In the seventies, those who seek basic social change have both the necessity and the opportunity to find a political strategy that can mesh with direct action and sociocultural experiment. To the extent that they fail to do this, it is likely that established political elements will find ways to manipulate the new consciousness that the sixties created. As I write this, evidence that professional politicians are trying to learn the language of youth is far more convincing than is evidence that radicalized youths are trying to learn the means to an effective political strategy.

The underlying argument of this chapter is that if the revolutionary aspirations of the youth revolt are to have a chance of fulfillment, the youth revolt must be transcended. It must be transcended, first, in the sense that the new consciousness that has been concentrated on the campus must spread to other locales and social groups, and that it must find ways of connecting to the needs and interests of the majority of Americans. It must be transcended, second, by finding ways for people who are filling adult roles—who are working and raising children—to act effectively for social and cultural change. What I have suggested so far is that such transcendence is possible through the collective action of GIs, young workers, and other nonstudent youth, through the establishment of youth-based communities and communes, through the women's liberation movement and related efforts to systematically remake intimate social relationships, through the collective action of young professionals and other "brainworkers" to fundamentally reorganize the meaning of their work and to create programs for social reconstruction, and through efforts to utilize the growing numerical power of youth and young adults to establish local coalitions for change and to form the basis for a national political party that can represent the new consciousness within the political system.

None of these trends is in itself "revolutionary," but, my feeling is that each of them is intrinsically significant, as I have tried to show. I argue that these trends contribute to a long-term *process* of revolutionary change in the society, a process whose outcome is impossible to predict.

Many of us tend to define revolution as a cataclysmic uprising, an insurrection that overthrows the government or gives rise to an all-out civil war. There was a time when hardly anyone believed that such an event could occur in an advanced industrial society such as the United States. On the one hand, most believed, people are too well-off to risk such a venture; on the other hand, the government is too powerful to make such a venture plausible. These days, given the decline in the legitimacy of the state and the intensity of social conflict of the past few years, most serious people would be far less confident about saying that insurrection or civil war is impossible in the United States.

In the past few years, many students have come to believe not only that this kind of revolution was not impossible, but that it was imminent. I think they based that feeling on the belief that a full-scale military crackdown on the ghettoes and the campuses was strongly likely, or that the United States government would continue to escalate the Vietnam war and bring on a desperate insurrection to stop it, or both. As I pointed out, the feeling that revolution or civil war was imminent receded during 1971. It did so, I believe, because the repressive thrust and escalatory impulses of the administration were largely blunted by a great variety of expressions of popular feeling.

In my opinion, it is healthy that student revolutionaries have come to realize the limitations of apocalyptic politics and have come to feel that the struggle will be prolonged and multifaceted. In fact, whether this society ever experiences a total breakdown, all-out civil strife, and internal warfare depends almost entirely on the actions taken by those in authority. One of the premises of this chapter is that a new period of liberal reform is likely to be ushered in with the 1972 presidential elections. Even now, under the Nixon administration, the president shows signs of realizing that he must move to the left rather than to the right on certain issues if he is to deal with political realities in this country.

It is possible that a reform-minded administration would be able to alleviate popular discontents and restore some of the eroded legitimacy of national authority. On the other hand, in a climate of reform, radical visions grow—although under these conditions, people may feel less receptive to the idea of otherthrowing the government.

In any case, the projections I have made here assume a climate of relative liberalism for the next few years. However, if the political system fails to reflect popular desires for change— if the Democrats nominate a candidate who is clearly identified as representing the old politics or if the interests and rights of blacks and other minorities, youth, and other insurgent groups are clearly denied and blocked by those in office, it is possible that the next years will be a period of intensifying and violent conflict, social breakdown, repression, and insurrection. At present, however, it seems more likely that the coming years will be characterized by a combination of conflict and accommodation rather than by total social cleavage.

WHY REVOLUTION?

In the introduction I said that in the past, emergence of large-scale youth revolt in a society has meant that the existing order is breaking down and that a new stage of history for that society is on the horizon. I think this is true for the United States in our time just as it was true for nineteenth century Russia, for China, and for Latin America. The cultural crisis that has dislocated so many young people is experienced by them as a problem of identity, of values, and of vocation. As I have observed, crisis is manifested in daily life by deep problems in the relations between parents and children, in the socialization of children and youth in school, and by a generally anomic social climate. One may ask the question: if the existing state of technology has made the traditional culture obsolete, why is it so hard to institute new values and a new cultural consensus in tune with that technology? The answer I would give requires more space than I have here, so I will state it as opinion. *The culture that is needed to mesh with our state of technological development is one that is incompatible with capitalism.* The culture that is struggling to be born stresses cooperation over competition, expression over success, communalism over individualism, being over doing, making art over making money, and autonomy over obedience. All these values are made possible by a technology that can eliminate much menial, hard, and boring work, can provide the means for decent living standards to all, and can provide the conditions for all members of society to develop fully their capacities for creativity, knowledge, self-expression and self-determination. All of these values are blocked by a social organization—corporate capitalism—requiring that energies be channeled into the making of money, that men work in order to secure their material well-being, and that a nation-state be militarily powerful and be based on class division and inequality.

In short, to have a new culture—and hence new life styles, new identities, and new freedoms—requires a new social organization. To establish such a postcapitalist, postindustrial, post-scarcity society would entail, by definition, a process of revolution.

Whether a revolutionary process must culminate in all-out warfare cannot, I think, be predicted. Whether it does depends almost entirely on those who hold political power. The revolutionary process, however, is not restricted to violent cataclysm; instead, it is a long, interconnected series of changes in consciousness, social relations, cultural patterns, and political behaviors.

Therefore, it seems appropriate to say that the revolution has already begun and that many of the trends I have suggested in this chapter represent important continuations of it.

Two conditions not now present seem to me crucial in the process of revolutionary change. First, a large body of people sharing both discontent and a self-conscious desire for change must organize and undertake deliberate activity of a political nature. They must be able to speak for, and eventually be supported by, the great majority of people. Second, the actions of those in revolutionary motion must be guided by a vision of the social order they hope to establish. These two conditions are interconnected. Without a mass movement of people who desire change, revolutionary proposals are empty utopias. But without a program, there cannot be either a substantial number of people willing to dedicate their lives to change or a majority of people willing to risk the security of the status quo for the uncertainties of a new society. Only a handful of people ever are eager to destroy the present without knowing something about what happens next—and these would be among the least wholesome persons to lead a movement.

These conditions take time to develop. I believe that if the kinds of efforts I have sketched in this chapter are seriously undertaken, these conditions could be brought into being.

The projections suggested in this chapter are based on the assumption that the spirit and energy of the youth revolt will continue to develop. I think that assumption is justified for a number of reasons.

First, the conditions that gave rise to the youth revolt are, if anything, more severe. The cultural crisis continues, and with it, the need to develop a new cultural framework. The counter-culture of the sixties has only begun the process of cultural transformation—only begun to find ways to implement new values in daily life. During the past few years, thousands of young people have acquired a sense of who they ought to be that is fundamentally incompatible with the conventional culture. These people, in myriad ways, certainly have deep needs to continue the quest for new ways of life. Some of the avenues they are likely to use have been suggested in this chapter.

Similarly, the crisis of the political system continues. Deep problems generate wide discontent; promises of their solution remain unfulfilled; increasingly, the populace feels that no leadership that can solve these problems exists today. Meanwhile, thousands of young people have experienced a political awakening and have developed commitments to dedicate their lives to basic change. Again, it seems to me, new possibilities to implement those commitments in the coming decade are opening up.

Thus, my analysis is optimistic: A society in deep historical crisis has reached the point where fundamental social and cultural transformation is necessary. That society, quite unwittingly, has produced a generation capable of making that transformation. The process of change has been, and will continue to be, painful, chaotic, and even bloody. Nevertheless, the material and technical potentialities of the society provide the ground for real breakthroughs in achieving the basis for equality, community and personal fulfillment—if the necessary structural changes can be brought about.

DISSOLUTION OF YOUTHFUL SOLIDARITY

I cannot conclude this essay on a note of unqualified optimism. There are ways in which the new consciousness is declining as well as flourishing. The sociocultural consciousness that began to develop during the past few years required, as I have emphasized, not only social crisis and personal discontent, but the *coming together* of youth. For an alternative culture and politics to grow and flourish, social solidarity must be maintained. One of the important features of American life however is that cohesive, fraternal, communal relations among people are very difficult to maintain.

Youth is the time of life when friendship, fraternity, and intimacy are most natural. As Erik Erikson has pointed out, one of the central tasks of youth is precisely to establish deep interpersonal relations—to learn who one is in relation to others, and to learn to love and care for those who are not blood relations. Moreover, as I have suggested, the establishment of solidarity among American youth was enormously facilitated by their incorporation into segregated enclaves, and the need for such solidarity was greatly strengthened by deepening problems of identity and alienation that many youth experienced.

School is one of the few *ready-made* settings for solidarity in our society. Thus, one of the key problems for the counter-culture and political radicalism as they move off the campus is to find and create new frameworks for bringing people together—for maintaining solidarity.

Why is solidarity so hard to achieve and why is it threatened among adherents of the new consciousness? I would postulate that most people have the wish to leave some mark of their having lived in the historical record. Perhaps a large component of human frustration is the result of a realization that few people make a contribution that makes their lives worthy of remembrance. Most of us learn to manage such frustration by raising a family; at least, by creating and raising children we have left a mark. The more ambitious and talented create artifacts—objects, ideas or events that become known to strangers or last beyond oneself. Still others find solace in religious visions of immortality.

Leaving a mark need not be an individual act. Certainly, one of the sources of energy for social movements is that they provide members with the sense of participation in the historic—they are *collective* means of leaving a mark.

One crucial aspect of industrial capitalism is that it has developed a culture that successfully channeled men's longing to leave a mark into the goal of occupational striving and monetary success. Of prime importance was the stress our culture put on *individual, competitive* achievement as the most valued means of obtaining recognition.

I have argued that the cultural emphasis on occupational and monetary achievement has broken down for large numbers of youth. This is one of the prime features of what I have called the cultural crisis and is one of the key factors contributing to youth movements of our time. However, I do not think the essential yearning for individual recognition has broken down. On the contrary. I think it is fair to say that rarely in history have so many young people been raised with the conviction that they had the right to uniqueness, that they were special, brilliant, deserving of recognition, and not fated to lead ordinary lives of quiet desperation. What they were not raised with was any clear sense of how to fulfill these promises of greatness. They were inculcated with the idea that they can and ought to leave a mark, but they were given very poor, confused, inadequate instruction about how to do it.

In our time mass media have become the primary route to *maximize* one's recognition, become famous, make history, leave a mark. The significance of the media in this regard has, I think, been little studied and understood—and I cannot pretend to rectify that situation here. But the channeling of yearnings for recognition through the mass media *has* become a central problem for sustaining a politics and culture of opposition and revolutionary change.

The innovators of the counterculture and the new left began without public recognition through the national media and in self-conscious opposition to the world portrayed on television, in the national mass magazines and newspapers, and in Hollywood movies. Probably they believed that recognition would come from specialized audiences, if they were artists, or from the political effects of their actions, if they were activists, and that it would come slowly and despite efforts by the commercial media to prevent it. Certainly, minstrels, musicians, and singers of the early sixties sought recognition, but more than that, they sought the satisfaction of being approved by a specially cognizant audience (I assume that this is what any serious artist hopes for). The early civil rights workers and other activists did not expect to be nationally famous as individuals. Rather they hoped that they would be admired for their courage and dedication by those who know them—and that their *acts* would have historical effect.

Much to their surprise, the youth vanguard was, in fact, rather quickly taken up by the national media. This was true first for the cultural innovators, who broke upon the scene just when the entertainment industry was rather desperate for new sources of material, and just when a mass market of youth with sophisticated taste was coming into flower.

By the mid-sixties, the new left was achieving a similar fame as television and magazines covered the increasingly large and dramatic demonstrations, writing up the new organizations, and selecting movement spokesmen for national attention.

Although movement activists were suspicious of the media and even of their new-found recognition, there was a noticeable shift of movement tactics and interests to capitalize on media coverage. Increasingly, movement members were self-conscious about the attention they received. They became aware of its value —the media offered an unparalleled means of having an impact on consciousness and events. For many, the staging of events to achieve coverage became a substitute for the previous emphasis on painstaking local organizing and face-to-face contact with potential recruits. The purest version of the politics of the mass media was exemplified by the yippies, who ingeniously created outrageous political happenings and persona and received the coverage they aimed for.

As I have suggested, this strategy worked. No question about it, television, records, *Life* magazine, and the press helped mightily to popularize the counterculture and the political resistance. But I argue here that the drive for media recognition has had damaging effects, particularly for maintaining the stable solidarity that a movement requires to achieve its long-term projects.

The basic problem with the media is their seductive power. They tend to greatly narrow the acceptable means for making and leaving a mark, and for having social and cultural impact. Consider the young poet, musician, artist, or writer who starts by getting joy out of the creative process itself and out of receiving recognition from his friends and others he can contact personally. Once he is seduced by the possibility of media recognition, joys of local audience are rarely adequate. Moreover, once local audiences are seduced by media stars, local artists are not good enough for them. The amateur's performance is second-rate; spontaneous creativity is a poor substitute for the magic of the superstar.

Similarly, the political activist might begin with a sense of the long-run importance of careful organizing, of local education, and of building stable organizations and institutions, but once he tastes the possibility that the "whole world is watching," such local work becomes boring, too slow, and meaningless compared with the instantaneous effects of confrontation, theatrical action, mass action, and violence.

Thus, the seduction of the media tends to dry up commitment to the building of local communities, of long-term cultural experiment, and of patient organizing. A second effect of the media is that they present overpowering models of identity. One of the obvious characteristics of youth is the search for viable models—for individuals whose lives and activities can serve as a basis for emulation. This is especially true in a time of cultural breakdown, when parents and other immediate elders provide little basis for emulation. The stuff of the media is composed of stars and heroes. And as the media have broadcast the virtues of youthful culture figures they have, more than ever before, created models for emulation. In particular, they have popularized the model of the romantic artist. Possibly, there are millions of youth whose heart's desire is to lead the life of the poet, the minstrel, or the free creative man—writing, playing, painting, and making films. But the structure of American mass communications will not permit millions to obtain media recognition. How many poets, novelists, musicians, filmmakers, muralists can an art and enter-tainment industry accommodate? Given the structure of capitalist society, how can mass aspirations to be creative be satisfied ex-cept through media recognition? One answer has been the ex-plosion of the so-called underground media—newspapers, film, and theater groups that have arisen out of the movement. But there is a limit even in the ability of the countermedia to absorb the available talent and they fail, in some respects, as adequate means of expression for either the movement or the individual creators.

The result, I believe, is a mass of young people with creative ambitions that are both heightened and frustrated and a conse-quent malaise in which jealousy, competitiveness, mistrust, and despair are prominent features. Not a very conducive climate for the flourishing of community, mutual support, and the patient building of countercultural institutions.

Further, the media not only popularize, but commercialize, countercultural symbols and sentiments. A counterculture, one feels, has maximum vitality when it can define itself in opposition and its symbols can be readily understood as standing for some-thing definable. One of the central ironies of the youth culture is that virtually all of the symbols, words, fashions, and experi-ments that were formulated in opposition to commercialism and business values have become marketable items, advertising gim-micks, and ways to make a buck. In this situation, symbols rapidly lose their specific meaning, the counterculture loses its sense of independence and opposition, and members lose the ability to distinguish true friend from exploiter.

The resulting paranoia is greatly reinforced by the fact that police surveillance personnel and *agents provocateurs* can adopt the fashions and styles of the counterculture almost as easily as merchandisers and media men can. When long hair becomes a cover for narcs and a means to sell hair spray, how long can it remain a symbol of brotherhood?

Finally, I believe that while the media contributes to the heightening and frustration of motives for fame, it offers a solution—namely, the idea that frustration can be obliterated through the passive consumption of pleasure. This idea has, of course, been intensely focused for this generation by the advent of pleasurable and mind-blowing drugs. Drugs, like the media, have had an ambiguous effect with respect to the new consciousness. Earlier, I stressed the positive effects of grass in spreading the youth culture and in creating conditions for radicalization of youth. But it may well be the case that drug use, and particularly the drug *scene,* is equally or ultimately a means for *draining* rather than for enhancing the energies necessary for concerted community building and action, and for encouraging passivity and tripping rather than concerted action.

There is little question that the tone of the youth movement, once liberated and exhilarating, has increasingly shifted toward despair. It would be silly to attribute this despair primarily to the seductions of the media and drugs, and the unadmitted and thrwarted drives for recognition that lie in the hearts of many youth. At bottom, the despair rests on the recalcitrance of the political system, on the resistance to real reform, on the increasing cost of political activism as governmental machineries of repression have been strengthened, and on the interminability of the Vietnam war.

But let me speculate one moment more about the sources of youthful despair. I think the whole argument of this essay can be boiled down to this: first the society created a new social type, called youth, and then provided very few ways for these new people to live in terms of the aspirations and feelings they developed. Youth has hope to the extent that it can believe that the future is open—open for social change, and open for personal opportunity.

The experience of this generation has been a dashing of hope that social change might come through moral pressure, persuasion, and example. More recently, middle class youth have come to experience what black and working class youth have had to face all along—the personal future is also profoundly blocked. College youth, having been raised with the conviction that education was a route to material security and to recognition, by the seventies, were discovering that their skills and talents were not as necessary as they had been led to believe. The freedom to experiment with identity, to refuse to accept undesirable work, to try out new vocations and life styles, and to freelance was unexpectedly closing down.

It was not that the country could not "afford" more teachers, doctors, scientists, lawyers, social workers, intellectuals, poets, and musicians. It was that the established priorities in governmental budgets, the established tax structure, the established balance between the public and private sectors necessitated the underemployment of people who had trained and aspired to work along these lines.

This situation could be more radicalizing than anything that has happened in the recent past has been. But, I am saying that it can also be profoundly demoralizing, as solidarity and political energy are drained by a scramble for scarce jobs—as experimental aspirations are suppressed because it is no longer so safe to take chances with one's future.

Contraction of the job market for educated youth is a prime cause for despair. When conventional jobs seemed plentiful, students felt they had time to search, to experiment, to drop out, to invent life styles. If one needed bread, one could always find something to do on the margin or, if necessary, could get back in—to graduate school, to teaching, or to social work, for example. Moreover, many politically active students felt that one could become a radical within the professions.

So the opportunity to develop a life style based on creativity and freedom from conventional restraints of adulthood—the opportunity to sustain such a life beyond studenthood—is challenged in two ways. On the one hand, it is undermined in an economic sense by contraction of the job market and the difficulties of living off one's creative work when there is an oversupply of artists. On the other hand, it is undermined in a psychological sense—by the unadmitted fear of anonymity and failure that can result if one is successful neither in a conventional career nor as a romantic artist who secretly yearns to be part of the media festival.

As long as leaving a mark is defined in media terms, most of us are fated for anonymity. As long as making history is defined in media terms, we are pressured to act theatrically and ultimately suicidally. In this situation, the decline of opportunity to gain recognition through conventional means such as teaching and professional work comes as an added, indeed a frightening, shock. The temptation to lose oneself completely, to give oneself over to passivity, to accept or escape chaos becomes considerable.

The fear that one is nothing and destined to be nothing is the dark side of trying to avoid the constraints of conventional adulthood. It is that fear that breaks the spirit of youth movements. Youth movements, by their very nature, cannot deal with this fear. This is especially true to the extent that the movement accepts the definitions established by the mass media of what recognition and making a mark mean.

The answer to such existential despair—if there is one—lies in the establishment of community. It lies in the mutual support of brothers and sisters in a common effort to construct a sensible life before the revolution. It lies in an effort to learn how collective work and action can be a more satisfying means of leaving a mark than is individual achievement. It lies in recovering the joy of creativity for its own sake and for the sake of one's local community. Finally it lies in the creation of a wider movement—encompassing men and women of all ages—a movement that provides a place for each in the remaking of society and permits people who lead conventional lives to contribute to the process of social change.

In the past few months, young people I have known have become murderers, have killed themselves, have drowned themselves in drugs, have become outlaws, have withdrawn into magic and mysticism, and have escaped to the woods. Others I have known are struggling to build self-determining communities, new institutions, new political organization—confronting with clear eyes the question of what next?

If I am optimistic, it is because we have a country that has a material base that is rich enough and a people who are discontented enough to make revolutionary change a viable possibility. It is because we have produced a mass of young people who despite all the ways in which they are confused, have so far demonstrated that they have the collective intelligence to lead such change. Finally, I think that some of what many of us have feared the most—a massive, brutal suppression of the forces of change—has, at least for the time being, been averted.

The idea of youth is a dangerous one for a social order, but it is also a very promising one. Youth revolt is a sign that a new culture and a new social order have been placed on the agenda of history. The promise of youth can only be fulfilled, however, if youth is transcended—if the young and the not-young who have a common interest in a new social order come together to make their collective mark and help cach other realize their common dreams.

BIBLIOGRAPHICAL NOTES

1. Figures I cite concerning the relative growth of the young adult population are derived from U.S. Bureau of the Census, *Statistical Abstracts, 1970* (Washington, D.C.: U. S. Government Printing Office, 1970), Table 7, "Current and Projected Population by Age and Sex: 1970–1990." The problem of unemployment among college graduates has been widely discussed and reported. An excellent continuing source of data is *Science,* the weekly publication of the American Association for the Advancement of Science.
2. The rise of radicalism among noncollege youth is illustrated in sources such as the following: Marc Liberle and Tom Seligson, *The Highschool Revolutionaries* (New York: Random House, 1970); James Birmingham, *Our Time is Now: Notes from the Highschool Underground* (New York: Bantam, 1970); Andy Stapp, *Up Against the Brass* (New York: Simon & Schuster, 1970); and Fred Gardner, *The Unlawful Concert* (New York: Viking Compass, 1970).
3. A vision of the political potentialities of youth ghettoes may be found in Tom Hayden, *Trial* (New York: Holt, Rinehart and Winston, 1970). A good practical review of alternative institutional development may be found in *The Organizers Manual*

(New York: Bantam Books, 1971). On communes, see Rosabeth Kanter, "Communes: Why and How They Are Formed; Which Are Likely to Make It and Why," *Psychology Today* (July 1970).

4. On the radicalization of educated labor—the journal *Social Policy* (International Arts and Sciences Press, 901 N. Broadway, White Plains, New York) is primarily devoted to analysis and criticism of movements for change within the "human services" professions. Detailed material on specific professional groups may be obtained from sources such as the following: Health Education Project, 202A N. Halsted St., Chicago, Ill. 60614. Medical Committee for Human Rights, 1520 Naudain St., Philadelphia, Pa. National Lawyers Guild, 1 Hudson St., New York, N.Y. Union of Concerned Scientists, PO Box 289, MIT Branch Station, Cambridge, Mass. 02139. New University Conference, 622 W. Diversey Blvd., Chicago, Ill. New York Media Project, PO Box 266, Village Station, New York, N.Y. The outstanding source of information on new vocations, alternative institutions, and new communities is: Vocations for Social Change *Newsletter,* Canyon, Calif. 94516.

5. A good source of material on the Women's Liberation Movement is Robin Morgan (ed.), *Sisterhood is Powerful* (New York: Random House, 1970). *Women: A Journal of Liberation* (3011 Builford Ave., Baltimore, Md.) is a good source of information, analysis, and discussion of problems of the women's movement.

6. An analysis of political behavior of youth that tends to play down the influence of radicalism is Seymour Martin Lipset, "Youth and Politics," in Robert K. Merton and Robert Nisbet, *Contemporary Social Problems,* Third Edition (New York: Harcourt Brace Jovanovich, 1971). Lipset's essay should be read by those who seek an antidote to the position I have taken in this essay. Lipset argues vigorously that the majority of youth "accept the system," that youthful radicalism is counterbalanced by youthful "backlashers," and that the developments of the sixties do not signify any necessity for basic social and cultural change.

7. My reflections on the problem of youthful solidarity and on the seductions of the mass media were stimulated by the work of Norman Fruchter, "Movement Propaganda and the Culture of the Spectacle," *Liberation* (May 1971).

8. An important statement on the possible new directions for the movement in the seventies is *New American Movement,* 1332 Oxford St., Berkeley, Calif. 94700.

INDEX

Activism
    emergence of student radical, 2–3, 73–96
    political, 136
Activist students, social origins of, 4–8, 79
Adolescence, 9–12
Adult backlash, 92, 103
Alienation, 43, 62, 64, 70, 72, 99, 121, 132
Altbach, Philip, 103
Ambivalence, parental, 22–23, 27–30
    See also Childrearing
American Medical Association, 114–15
Anomie, 22, 35, 47–48, 110
Antiwar movement, 84, 88, 108, 120
Ariès, Philippe, 9, 19
Authority, 24, 32
    delegitimation of, 96 99, 128
    parental, 24, 55–56
Aya, Rod, 102

Backlash, adult, 92, 123
Backward societies, emergence of generational conflict in, 11–15
Baez, Joan, 62, 63
Bales, Robert F., 34
Beach Boys, 63
Beatles, 67, 70

Ben-David, Joseph, 19
Berger, Bennett, 19
Berkeley (California), 82–83, 111–12
    as a bohemian subculture, 109
    effects on reform, 82–83
    elections (1970), 121
    elections (1971), 122
Birmingham, James, 139
Black militance, 90, 109
Black militants, 85
Black Panther Party, 90, 94
Black student movement, 74–75
Black student unions, 90
Bohemianism, student, 3, 6, 16–17, 107–14
Breakdown, cultural, 41
Bureaucracy, growth of, 36–37
Byrds, The, 63

Cambodia, invasion of, 92, 94
Campus
    during the 1950s, 52
    military crackdown on, 127–28
    political groups on, 2–3
    revolt on, 116
    spread of new consciousness from, 126
Capitalism
    changes in, 35
    corporate, 129
    cultural framework of, 22

entrepreneurial, 35
and higher education, 38
incompatibility of with new culture, 129
place of middle class in, 33
Capitalist culture, 119
Childrearing, 20–34, 47, 111, 113
conflict between freedom and permissiveness, 25–26
parental value conflict and confusion, 25–30
CIA (Central Intelligence Agency), activities in student organizations, 86
Civil disobedience, 77, 91, 93
Civil rights movement, 76–79, 120
Clark, Burton, 102
Class consciousness, 116–17
Clinics, free, 114
Cohen, Albert, 102
Cohn, Nick, 103
Coleman, James, 102
Collective living, 110–11
Collins, Randall, 19
Columbia University (1968), 88
"Coming together" of youth, 131
Communes, 110–11, 113–14, 127
rural, 113–14
Communications, 48
Communist party, 74
Confusion, parental, 25–27
Consciousness
collective, of youth, 44, 48, 49–53, 101
community, in youth ghettoes, 111
See also New consciousness
Conscription. See Draft
Cook, Bruce, 102
Corporate capitalism, 129
Counterculture, 17, 47, 48, 104–5, 110, 117, 120
Counterinstitutions, 110, 112, 113, 120
Credibility gap, 97
Crisis
cultural, 129, 130, 132

identity, 41, 47–48, 129, 132
Cuban invasion (Bay of Pigs), 79
Cuban missile crisis, 79
Cuban revolution, 75
Cultural incoherence, 18, 33, 35, 47
Cultural transformation, 112
Culture
alienated, 70
coherence of, 22–23
crisis in, 129, 130, 133
diffusion of, 60–72
"prefigurative," 72
youth, 17–18, 95
See also Counterculture

Defense establishment, 83
Delegitimation
of national authority, 96–98
of political system, 89
Democratic Convention
of 1964, 80–81, 88, 89
of 1968, 88, 89
of 1972, 123
Deviant subculture, 95
Diffusion
cultural, 109
process of, 60–73
Disillusionment, 13–14
Dissent
in the military, 107–8
in the nonmilitary, 108–9
Doors, the, 63
Draft, 97
conscript army, 43–44, 48
conscription, 86
student deferments, 42
Dropouts, 110
Drugs, 68–69
effects of, 136
mood-manipulating, 68
psychedelic, 68
Dylan, Bob, 62, 63, 71

East Village, 109
Economic insecurity, 106

Education, higher, 106
  and capitalism, 38
  consequences of, 39–42, 54–56
  functions of, 38–41
  mass, rise of, 36–38, 48
  and social change, 10–19
Eighteen year old vote, 94, 111, 112
  impact of on constituency, 121–22
Eisenhower, Dwight D., 75
Eisenstadt, Smuel N., 19
Equality, sexual, 111
Erikson, Erik, 31, 102, 131
Establishment of community, 138
Establishment, resistance to reform, 12–13
Extended family, dissolution of, 23–24

Family
  extended, 23–24
  nuclear, 23, 25, 26, 119
  structural change in, 23–32
  See also Childrearing
Faris, R. E., 19
Fascism, 73
Fashions
  influence of Beatles on, 66–67
  major elements of youth culture, 66–68
  meanings of change in, 67
  unisex, 67
FBI (Federal Bureau of Investigation), 94
Feminism, new, 119
Feuer, Lewis, 15, 19
Films, 65
Fisher, Eddie, 62
Flacks, Richard, 19, 102, 103
Folk culture, 57
Fortune Magazine survey, 87
Free Speech Movement, Berkeley, 82–83
  See also Berkeley
Free university, 82, 83

Freedom Democrats of Mississippi (1964), 80–81
Friedan, Betty, 34
Friedland, W., 46
Fruchter, Norman, 140

Gardner, Fred, 139
Generational conflict, 11–19, 47, 89–90, 98
Generational equilibrium, 15
"Generational units," 51
Ghettoes
  military crackdown on, 127–28
  urban, 120
  See also Youth ghettoes
Gintis, H., 46
GIs, 107–9, 127
Goldsen, Rose, 102
Government spending, cutbacks in, 106
Green, A. W., 34
Greensboro, N. C., sit in (1960), 74–76
Greenwich Village, as bohemian refuge in thirties, 16
Group consciousness, music as expression of, 64
Guerilla action, 92–93, 99

Haight-Ashbury (San Francisco), 68, 109
Hayden, Tom, 139
Hershey, Lewis, 85
Hickel, Walter, 97
Higher education. *See* Education, higher
"Hippie," culture, 68
  as a target of abuse, 67
Hollingshead, August, 102
Hopkins, Jerry, 103
Horowitz, Irving, L., 46
Hughes, H. Stuart, 77
Humanistic models of man, 115
Humphrey, Hubert, 88
Hungary (1956), 74

Identity
  crisis, 41, 47–48, 129, 132
  formation, 49–50
  problems, 50–51
Incoherence
  cultural, 35, 47
  patterns of, 33
Intellectual culture, diffusion of,
    60–72
Intellectual subculture as deviant,
    56–60
Intellectual youth, 52–54
  culture, 95
  estrangement of, 16–17, 52
Intimidation, 118
Isla Vista (California), 111–12
Isolation of students, 99–100

Jackson State College, 91, 94
Jagger, Mick, 63
James, Joni, 62
Jazz era, 61
Jefferson Airplane, 63
Jencks, Christopher, 19, 46
Johnson, Lyndon B., 108
  administration, 80, 84
Joplin, Janis, 63

Kanter, Rosabeth, 140
Keniston, Kenneth, 19, 34, 55, 58,
    102, 103
Kennedy, John F., 99
  administration, 78–79
  assassination, 80
Kennedy, Robert F., 81, 87–88
Kent State University, 91, 94, 99
Khrushchev, Nikita, 74
King, Martin Luther, Jr., 74–75,
    76, 88

Labor force, 37–38
  mobility of, 23–24
  upgrading of, 43

Laufer, Robert S., 103
Law and order, as a political issue,
    92, 125
Legal centers in urban ghettoes,
    115
Leisure, 37
Lennon, John, 63
Liberalism, political climate of, 128
Liberation movement, youth, sepa-
    ratist, 118
Liberle, Marc, 139
Life style, 64
  challenged, 137–38
  humanistic, 111
  nuclear family, 111
Lindsay, John, 97
Lipset, Seymour Martin, 19, 34,
    140
Lowenstein, Allard M., 122
Lowenthal, Leo, 34

McCarthy "children crusade," 87–
    88
McCarthy, Eugene, 61, 87–88, 97,
    99, 122, 123
McCarthyism of the fifties, 2
McClelland, David C., 34
Mailer, Norman, 57, 102
Male-centeredness of youth move-
    ment, 117
Manipulation, 64–65, 118
Mannheim, Karl, 51, 102
March on the Pentagon (1967), 86
March on Washington (1963), 80
March on Washington (1965), 86
Marijuana, 68, 69, 70, 71
  as symbol of defiance, 69
  use of in the military, 107
Marx, Karl, 42–43, 117
Mass consciousness, 48
Mass higher education. *See* Educa-
    tion, higher
Mass media, 44, 69–70, 133–34
  impact of, 45
  politics of, 134–35
  and youth vanguard, 133

Mass movements, communication in, 36
Matza, David, 19, 103
Mead, Margaret, 72
Media, mass. *See* Mass media
Media, underground, growth of, 135
Merton, Robert K., 140
Militance
  Black, 90, 109
  intensification of, 87
  labor, 94
  student, 92–93
Miller, Daniel, 34
Miller, Norman, 102
Mills, C. Wright, 79
Mississippi Summer Project, 80
Morgan, Robin, 140
Music
  bluegrass, 62
  country and western, 63
  folk, 62
  hard rock, 87
  jazz, 61
  new, 61–66
  rhythm and blues, 62
  rockabilly, 62
  song lyrics, 64
  soul, 63
  and youth protest, 64

Nader, Ralph, 99
Nationalism, 13–14
Nationwide student strike, 91–92
New consciousness, 132
  media effect on, 136
  spread of, 107–9, 116–17
New feminism, 119
New left, 48, 78–79, 110, 133–34
New left activists, social origins of, 4–8
New leftists, 104–5
New politics, 61
Newcombe, Theodore, 102
Nisbet, Robert, 140
Nixon, Richard M., 88, 108, 128

Nonviolent movement, 74–75
Nuclear family, 23, 25, 26, 111, 119

O'Brien, James J., 103

Pacifist action, 76
  See also Antiwar movement
Page, Patti, 62
Paris, as bohemian refuge in twenties, 16
Parsons, Talcott, 34, 102
Peace Corps, 80
Peer culture, 49–50, 59
Peer group, 72
Personal discontent, 131
Personal identity, establishment of, 100–1
Police harassment, 110
Police surveillance, 136
Political action of youth, 127
Political disaffiliation, student, 74
Political indifference of American students, 74
Political party
  formed by American radicalization, 125
  new, of the left, 123–24
  See also Black
  Panther Party
Political radicalism, 16, 17, 94–95
Political style, change in, 123
Political system, crisis of, 130–31
Politics, workings of, 126
Populist movement, 73
Pot. *See* Marijuana
President's Commission on Campus Unrest (*Report*), 103
Protest
  activity by military, 108
  music of, 87
Protestant Ethic, 20, 22, 25, 33, 71
  causes of changes in, 21
  decline of, 71–72
  and women, 21

Racial crisis, 97
Radical political alliances, 124–25
Radicalism, political, 16–17, 94–95
Radicalization, 89–90
    intensification of, 87
    of students, 85–87
    of youth, 120
Radical-populist-socialist political organizations, 125–26
Radicals in the professions, 114–17
Reagan, Ronald, 92
Reform, government resistance to, 136
Registration, voter, 121
Relationships, social, 112
Resistance, organized, in the military, 84
"Revisionist" interpretation of American history, 115
Revolt, collective
    music as expression of, 64
    reasons for, 6–7
Revolutionaries, student, 104–5, 128
Revolutionary change, process of, 130
Revolutionary commitment, 90
"Revolutionary" logic, 107
Revolutionary social change, process of, 127
Riesman, David, 19, 34, 46
Role confusion, 31–32
Rowntree and Rowntree, 46

Sanford, R. Nevitt, 46, 102
Schumpeter, Joseph, 34
Seligson, Tom, 139
Sex role
    definitions, 58–59
    revolt, 117–19
Shils, Edward, 19
"Silent majority," 93
Sklar, Martin, 102
Skolnick, Jerome, 103

Slater, Philip, 34
Social change, pace of, 30–34
Social crisis, 131
Social disorganization, 110
Social reform, fundamental, 115–16
Social relationships, efforts to remake, 127
Socialist movement, 73
Sociocultural consciousness, 131
Sociocultural crisis, youth revolt as symptom of, 6
Solidarity, dissolution of youthful, 131–39
Stalinism, 73
Stapp, Andy, 139
Street people, 110
Structural transformations, 48
Student movement, 95, 116
    absence of, in capitalist countries, 14–15
    effect of Berkeley on, 82
Student Non-violent Co-ordinating Committee (SNCC), 75, 76, 80
Student protest
    decline of, 99–101
    history of, implications of, 94–96
Students, economic insecurity in college, 105–6
Students for a Democratic Society (SDS), 3–4, 78, 80, 84, 87, 88, 90, 91, 93
    demise of, 91
Subculture
    bohemian, 109
    campus alternative, 56–58
    "delinquent," 52
    deviant, 95
    intellectual, 57, 59
    intellectual, parental characteristics of, 54–56
    youth, 51–52
Success, 31
Swanson, Guy, 34

Taylor, James, 63
Teach-ins, 84
Technological development, 37
Teodori, Massimo, 103
Third parties, radical, 125–26
Tonkin, Gulf of, resolutions, 84
Trow, Martin, 102

Underground art, appearance in
  mass-circulation magazines,
  65
Underground media, 135
Underground newspapers, military,
  107–8
Unemployment
  of educated youth, 106, 137
  of Vietnam veterans, 108
Unions, of professionals, 117
University
  as an alternative culture, 83
  reform, 83–84
  student challenge to, 100
Urban ghettoes, 48, 120
Urban guerillas, 91

Value system, conventional American, 49–50
Vietnam war, 84, 97, 107–8, 123,
  127 28, 136
  university perspective on, 84–85
  veterans, 107–8
Vocational training, 37

Wallace, George, 109
Weathermen (faction of SDS), 93
Weber, Max, 20, 34
White, Winston, 34
Williams, Paul, 103

Women's Liberation movement,
  94, 117–19, 127

Yippies, 134
Young voter, emergence of, 123–
  25
Youth
  alienated intellectual, 53–54
  increase in number of, 105
  intellectual, 53–54
  meaning of, in American Soci-
    ety, 104–7
  middle class deviant, 52–53
  nonstudent, 107–9, 127
  public hostility to, 92
  segregation of, 9–11, 69. *See
    also* Youth ghettoes
  uncommitted, 58
  voting as a bloc, 122
Youth culture, 47–103
  elements of, 60–73
  functions of, 49–60
  male-centeredness, 117–18
  political and social role of, 111–
    14
Youth ghettoes, 91, 94, 109–14
  community consciousness in,
    111–12
  Isla Vista (California), 111–12
Youth movement, 132, 138
  despair in, 136
  male-centeredness, 117 18
  women's role in, 117–19
Youth revolt, 126, 130
Youth vanguard, and mass media,
  133
Youth vote
  American political changes
    caused by, 122–26
  potential, 121–24